To Leonard Shaykin

Making the Most of Your Life!

A Love Letter to My Grandchildren

By

Bud Shuster, MC, Ret.

With best wishes!

Bud Shuster

RAGGED EDGE PRESS
SHIPPENSBURG, PENNSYLVANIA

The photographs were provided by the author.

This Ragged Edge Press publication
was printed by
Beidel Printing House, Inc.
63 West Burd Street
Shippensburg, PA 17257-0708 USA

The acid-free paper used in this book meets the guidelines for permanence and durability of the Committee on Production Guidelines for Book Longevity of the Council on Library Resources.

For a complete list of available publications
please write
Ragged Edge Press
Division of White Mane Publishing Company, Inc.
P.O. Box 708
Shippensburg, PA 17257-0708 USA

PRINTED IN THE UNITED STATES OF AMERICA

To

My Grandchildren:

Bobby, Ali, Megan, Garrett, Emily,
Greg, Will, Michael, Andrew, Jonathan,
Daniel, Jack—their children,
and their children's children

The twelve grandchildren at Shuster Lodge

Contents

Foreword

Hugh Sidey, *Time* magazine's distinguished Washington Contributing Editor, wrote that Bud Shuster's "remarkable journey to the U.S. Congress is the stuff of the dream." But, I can report, having been Bud's close friend since we were boys, that his entire life is the stuff of the dream.

Although Bud's book is written for his grandchildren as a guide to achieving a productive and meaningful life, nearly everyone—parents, grandparents, young and old—can profit from the lessons of his extraordinary life.

His boundless energy, enthusiasm, and positive approach to life make it easy to forget that he started out in the bleakest of times with little more than the love of his family and a fierce dedication to making his life count. Yet he has never lost that quality that lets people, from blue-collar workers to national leaders, feel comfortable in his presence.

Bud's broad range of experiences has given him an insight into the many faces of America and the world—more than most will ever know.

While the highlights of his life properly paint a portrait of an accomplished leader, this book also lets us feel the warmth and love inside his soul.

—Dr. Mark C. Nagy

Introduction

The love, encouragement, and gentle guidance I received from my family as I grew up made an enormous impact on me. So I decided to pass along the benefit of my life's experiences to our little ones and others who might find them useful.

I am fortunate to have led a full life. I was born an American in a time of opportunity and abundance. I am healthy and energetic (with what our children call "the Shuster engine").

My family gave me roots and a desire to make my life worthwhile. I achieved my boyhood dream of becoming a United States congressman, representing constituents for nearly three decades who let me vote my conscience and chairing the largest congressional committee in history to rebuild America. And as the ranking member of the Select Intelligence Committee, I participated in some of the most momentous intelligence decisions of our time.

In sum, I have lived a life for which I give thanks as being beyond what any man could claim as his due. At the same time, I have learned enough to know that life does not stand still; that no one escapes difficult times. What matters is how we face such times. I have been privileged to witness many examples of fortitude. My dear mother, who lost her legs as a result of a blood clot, personified courage and the best of human qualities. And yet her suffering somehow made her stronger. She rose to light the lives of others when she could no longer stand. I, too, have experienced setbacks and disappointments. But I'm blessed that when my neck was broken in a car accident, I made a full recovery. I also have a family I am proud of and who gives me unconditional love.

This book is a love letter for my grandchildren. It is one that goes beyond simply saying the words "I love you" (for they already know that), to sharing with them both my public and private, even intimate, observations on how they can make the most of their lives.

Although I picture twelve young children as I write, I know too well how life moves swiftly on; how twelve years from now, they will be teenagers or young adults making their own decisions about how to live each day.

We can seize all that life has to offer or simply stumble through. I believe this book will help you make daily decisions and design your life plans from lessons I have learned—often the hard way—sometimes temporarily forgotten, and, on occasion, neglected to practice.

Although we sometimes fail to heed our own advice, we must always try. Whenever I have followed my better instincts, the positive results have usually surpassed my fondest expectations. Imperfect though we are, when we carefully define our goals and discipline ourselves to work toward them, we sometimes even touch our dreams.

Chapter One
Believing

It is not wisdom to be only wise...but it is wisdom to believe the heart.

—Santayana

I was only eleven years old, tramping through the deep, new snow. I couldn't know that the next few minutes would profoundly affect my life and the lives of countless others. Tucked tightly under my left arm was an old hand-painted shaving mug, carefully wrapped with tissue paper inside a brown paper bag. It was 1943. My dear grandfather, the town's barber, recently had died. Except for a collection of shaving mugs, there was little of value in his half-century-old barbershop. Painted by my grandmother, Nana, around the turn of the century, each mug featured its own individual flowery design and bright color scheme, with the patron's name ornately lettered in the center. For years the mugs had been good only for decoration on the barbershop's shelves. The days had long since passed when men got lathered out of shaving mugs for a straight-razor shave.

While cleaning out the shop, Nana had come across the mug that had belonged to Asa Weiss, a Jewish immigrant who had died without knowing that one day his son, Sammy, would be elected to the Congress of the United States. Congressman Weiss lived only two blocks from us, and Nana thought he would be pleased to have this memento of his father.

Apprehensive about knocking on the congressman's door, yet excited at the thought, I set out on my errand on that cold December night, at a time when our little Pennsylvania town, along with the rest of America, ached. Nearly half the houses along the way displayed small, red-bordered white banners in their front windows. Most had a blue star in the center, indicating that someone from that family was serving in the military. Some had a silver star, meaning he was overseas, and one, a gold star, meaning he wasn't coming home.

I thought about the congressman who traveled back and forth to Washington each week, helping make decisions that surely would win an awful war. There could be no doubt. In my innocent world, good always triumphed over evil, and the difference between the two was always clear to see. I remembered the day a few months after Pearl Harbor was bombed when I stood on my tiptoes among the crowd on the corner of Monongahela Avenue with my grandfather in front of his barbershop watching the first round of draftees being loaded onto streetcars—more streetcars than I had ever seen. Young men were standing in the aisles and hanging out of the windows. The streets were jammed too, but the townspeople craning to see were eerily silent, except for a few sobs and the wails of one Polish mother in her black babushka who chased after her son's streetcar as it pulled away. The congressman was there, standing on a bunting-draped flatbed truck with a half-dozen other prominent citizens, looking as serious as undertakers, waving wordlessly.

I remembered how that summer I had stood behind the bench at an old-timers baseball game as the congressman rushed through the gate pounding his glove and apologizing for being late. He had just arrived from Washington, he said, where they had been pushing emergency war measures through the Congress. To me, Washington was the center of the world, and, yet, here he was, one of us, with his battered glove, rolled-up pants, and faded sweatshirt.

To the townspeople, he was more than a congressman, more than the highest elected official who had ever come out of Glassport, our small town, fourteen miles south of Pittsburgh. He was hope— the link, our lifeline, with the fearsome world beyond; he was the one

Bud, *center*, with his buddies

last person to whom we could turn for help when all else failed; and turn to him our townsfolk did—by the hundreds. He was our protector—the one man with both the power to make things happen and heart enough to care. He did more for our community than even our priests and preachers. And I was on my way to give him a very special gift—something that couldn't be purchased in a store.

When I arrived, I seated myself on one of the wooden straight-backed chairs in his outer office. Through the thin wall, I caught the rhythm of the procession in and out of the congressman's office. An ashen-faced woman whose ragged black dress hung beneath her tattered coat asked in broken English if her only son might be brought home from overseas because her husband had died. The corner service-station owner talked of how he needed his gas allotment increased to fulfill the requirements of his customers. The high-school halfback, sitting with his parents, explained why he wanted to go to West Point. To those and many more, the congressman listened and said he would try to help.

When it came my turn to see him that night, I took a deep breath as I entered his office, delivered the speech I had rehearsed in my head, and handed him Nana's gift.

Placing the mug on a nearby shelf, he told me how much it meant to have a remembrance of his father, tousled my hair, and said, waving a friendly finger at me, "You grow up to be as good as your grandfather, and you'll be quite a man!"

Beaming, I shuffled backward out of the office, too excited to even turn around, pulled my wool cap down over my ears, and with my heart thumping wildly, ran down the steps onto the icy pavement and into the dark, snowy night.

Although the cold, raw wind stung my face, the afterglow of my encounter filled me with a mellow warmth. It had been the most exciting few moments of my young life. For an instant, my world—a worn-out fuliginous valley of dreary steel mills and frightened people—had been transmuted into a magical room where a single person possessed the ability to right the wrongs being inflicted on good people all about him.

As I neared my home, I stopped suddenly, knee-deep in snow, and earnestly announced aloud to the stars in the frigid winter sky: "Someday I'm going to be a congressman!"

Thirty years later, my boyhood dream came true. Flanked by my five children in the chamber of the U.S. House of Representatives, with my wife, Patty, and my cousin Sylvia in the family gallery, I raised my right hand to take the oath of office as a duly elected member of the Congress of the United States.

By believing in my dream and believing in myself, my dream had become a reality.

* * *

I was lucky. I learned to believe in myself because, from the time I was a small child, the people around me—my parents, grandparents, older cousins, aunts and uncles—gave me their unconditional love. *They* believed in me. I remember Nana telling me as a little kid—actually drumming it into me—"You've got personality plus, Kiddo!" I didn't even know what that meant. Rather than my really having it, she was injecting it in me.

My uncle Bill Zeigler gave me a dime for every A on my report card, stimulating my competitive drive. Cousin Sylvia gave me piano lessons from the time I was five, which meant that from the first grade on, my teachers counted on me to lead my classmates in various musical programs. I felt special, and that gave me confidence.

Another cousin, Lloyd, who had been a great athlete—a semi-pro football player and boxer, in addition to being a tough policeman and my Sunday-school teacher—had immersed me in sports. He taught me how to throw a curveball and took me on my first swim across the Monongahela River (much to my mother's chagrin). That gave me more self-assurance. My parents and grandparents saw to it that I participated in church plays. Performing in front of an audience instilled even more self-confidence.

Although we were only of modest means, clean clothes, good manners, and proper English were absolute requirements. Words

Bud performs in a high-school concert

like "ain't" and "you'ens" and bad habits like dirty hands or shoes, or elbows on the table brought swift rebukes. It seemed a real bother at the time, but I think the attention and concern gave me a strong sense of self-worth.

The encouragement ingrained in me a positive outlook on life, a feeling that if I approached a situation with enthusiasm, I could achieve any goal I set.

And I learned that some things can come too easily. The ability to get good grades in school without trying too hard was a confidence builder, but I regret that I didn't study harder. I could have learned much more. And I later found that success in life is very much related to what you learn. I certainly had to play catch-up in college.

The day Dr. Hickes, our high-school principal, called me into his office to inform me that I had won the academic scholarship to the University of Pittsburgh, he sat me down and in his gruff, authoritarian manner said, "Shuster, you've won the Pitt scholarship. I probably made a big mistake by recommending you. You're going to go up there and think you can slide by, getting good grades without studying, like you've done around here. And you'll flunk out. A more deserving student could have, and probably should have, been awarded this scholarship. You'll be an embarrassment to this school, to your family, to the whole town, and to yourself—that is if you'll have sense enough to realize it. Congratulations! You'll be getting a letter from the university. Now get out of here."

As I ran the half-block home to tell my family, I was overjoyed. It meant I would be entering a great university instead of a dreary steel mill. But I was hurt by the way he had talked to me. And I was angry. By God, I'd show that little runt! I would not only survive, I'd excel at Pitt. He'd fired my competitive spirit. I'd make everyone proud of me, and to hell with him!

Our varsity basketball coach, who also was our health teacher, was a taskmaster both on the court and in the classroom. This was the same coach who had caught me smoking on the street corner in my sophomore year, and had said, "Shuster, you can smoke or you

Bud (number 8) on the high-school championship basketball team

can play basketball for me, but you can't do both." (I never smoked another cigarette.) He had taught us how to prepare class outlines in meticulous detail. I dug out my old health class notes to use as a guide for outlining my college classes. As a freshman at Pitt, I studied during my free time through the day and almost every evening from 7 to 11 PM, re-outlining the notes I took in class. After reading and underlining our textbook assignments, I outlined what I had read to fix it clearly in my head.

At the end of my first semester, when I got my grades, I jumped in my jalopy, sped straight to my high school, took the steps two at a time, and marched into the principal's office demanding to see him. When he came out and stood on the other side of the counter, staring at me quizzically, I slapped my transcript down in front of him: four A's and a B.

He grinned and cocked his head sideways, which was one of his mannerisms, and blurted out, "Well, it looks like you've learned to straighten out and fly right, young man." A few weeks later, when I was elected to the freshman scholastic honor society, I knew I was on my way.

Prior to the start of the semester, in September, we freshmen had been herded off to an orientation week at a camp located in Western Pennsylvania's foothills. Sitting around a campfire on the final night, we heard from the graduate who had been named the outstanding senior of his class the previous year—the kind of person the "university aims to produce in scholarship, character, and leadership." Each year the recipient's name was chiseled in a large stone along the campus walk.

The outstanding young man, who had been captain of the university's varsity debating team, told us that our next four years could be the most important, most formative years of our lives. He explained that we could become either "streetcar students" who returned home as soon as classes ended each day or students who threw ourselves into campus life, thereby gaining the full measure of a college education. I listened intently in the shadows of the flickering fire. As I weighed his words exhorting us to make the most of college and studied the faces of my new classmates, I set my four-year goal: to be named the outstanding senior of the class of 1954.

Never mind that I was the product of a small mill town's public school system and would be competing with students from many of America's most highly rated public and private schools. Never mind that I had never set foot inside that university, or any other, before that week. Never mind that I decided on the spot that, like the camp-fire speaker, I would become a college debater even though I had never even heard a debate, let alone participated in one. The chal-lenge, the very audacity of my dream, energized me. I *believed* I could do it!

And I did. Four years later, I had been elected to Phi Beta Kappa, served as president of several campus organizations, and won the Grand National Intercollegiate Debating Championship along with my partner, Lloyd Fuge. That June, I stood in silent awe as my name was engraved upon the university's campus walk.

The dream I had embraced around the freshman campfire had come true. I had believed I could do it. But believing was only the beginning. I had converted my belief into a number of smaller goals and had set out to achieve them. For example, to make the junior varsity debate team, I had more than met the coach's requirement to submit an outline of that year's national collegiate debate topic dealing with fair employment practices. My paper was a footnoted, detailed analysis of both sides of the issue. The coach singled it out for its thoroughness in front of the whole team.

The following year, when the varsity debaters stumbled in sev-eral tournaments, the coach promoted two of us, giving me the op-portunity to participate in major tournaments around the country—eventually leading to the Grand National Debate Tourna-ment. Winning that event splashed my picture, along with headlines and a front-page story, across the *Pitt News.* That never would have happened had I not resolved to make the team and then worked hard to produce that first report. And defining and attacking sub-goals is a formula I've followed successfully throughout my life.

During my college years I discovered that each of my efforts returned many times the cost, that the satisfaction from achievement

Pitt championship debate team: Balles, Reese, Purdy, Shuster

made the tasks worthwhile. I learned that a dream is a goal you give your heart to; that a goal is a dream with muscle added.

It was as if I'd discovered one of the world's great mysteries— that you can accomplish what you want by believing you can; that believing in yourself can set events in motion. Over the years I have seen it borne out time and again.

I also learned that not all dreams come true. Until I was a teen-ager, I wanted to be a major league baseball player but realized that I didn't have that level of talent. Simply wishing for something isn't enough to make it happen. You need to define the outer limits of your reach, and then focus on achieving it.

I also learned that even unfulfilled dreams have a way of branch-ing into new possibilities. Positive beliefs sometimes unlock new challenges. And even when an important goal comes head to head with a stubborn immovable reality, it finds new paths that lead to other opportunities, just as water splashing against a rock is diverted in different directions. Throughout my life, I never lost my sense of wonder each time a dream came true. I never fully understood it, but I couldn't doubt what I repeatedly experienced.

I'm certainly not the first person to discover the power of belief. It has figured strongly since biblical times, extending from theologi-cal to psychological experiences, from physical to intellectual achieve-ments. Although skeptics may dismiss belief as nothing more than a psychological trick that people use to motivate themselves, the evi-dence of its power is rooted both in the works of the great philoso-phers and in modern-day science.

Studies indicate that belief actually can cause the brain to re-lease pain-fighting chemicals. Today, hypnosis is used in medical procedures, from childbirth to weight control and drug addiction. Dr. Jerome Frank, professor emeritus of psychiatry at Johns Hopkins Medical School, wrote: "Our beliefs determine our behavior. Faith heals. Negativism destroys. Man must believe to make sense of life."

Believing, for me, has been an engine that has driven me to achieve my dreams.

I remember sitting as a pledge in front of a tribunal of fraternity brothers, hoping to pass the final test so I could be initiated into the Sigma Chi brotherhood at Pitt. "What is your goal in life?" one of them demanded. Hesitating, I stammered, "To make my life worthwhile."

"Not to live a happy life?" another of the brothers asked.

"Sure, everyone wants to live a happy life," I shrugged, timidly. "But I think it's more important to make sure your life counts for something, to make some kind of a contribution, to...to make your life worthwhile," I repeated.

To me, that meant doing things that seemed to have value: being healthy, financially secure, sharing my life with a loving family and friends, expanding my knowledge, and living in a country that prizes freedom tempered with personal responsibility. A life where, when I meet my maker, I could say: "Forgive me for my many sins and failures, for I have tried to the very best of my ability to do my duty and make my life worthwhile."

That question, put to me so many years ago, is one of the first and most important questions you have to answer for yourself. What do you want to aim for in life? For your life to be meaningful, it must be made up of goals that develop as you grow and mature. But before you set them, you must first decide what *you* believe. If you don't decide that—refining, adjusting, and even changing your beliefs as you learn and experience life's lessons—you won't be maximizing your opportunities in life. I can tell you what I believe, what I've learned in my lifetime, in the hope that it will help you live a rich, full life. But only you can decide what values you cherish and how you're going to organize and dedicate your life to achieving your goals.

Becoming a U.S. congressman meant that I could give my life value by helping thousands of people with individual problems and building up our region, our state, and the nation. My opportunities exceeded my imagination. By becoming chairman of the Transportation & Infrastructure Committee, the largest committee in the history of Congress, I was able to push through historic legislation to build and improve America's highways, public transit, aviation, economic development, railroads, flood control, ocean shipping, and clean water systems.

Once when I was touring a small rural community in Central Pennsylvania, a lady came up to me and said, "God bless you, Congressman. For the first time in many years, I can turn on the spigot in my kitchen and not get dirty water, thanks to the new community water system you got funded for us." On a much grander scale, passing TEA-21 to unlock the Highway Trust Fund meant that America's transportation system would be improved, ultimately saving lives that would have been lost in car accidents.

As the ranking member on the Select Intelligence Committee, I was able to craft legislation to improve our nation's security, creating a classified electronic air-to-ground system that was used to bring down drug lords in South America and save our soldiers' lives in the first Gulf War.

These are tangible examples of work that has made my life meaningful. But it is an incomplete list. John Foster Dulles, secretary of state under President Dwight D. Eisenhower, said, "No success in public life can adequately compensate for failure in the home." Raising well-balanced, responsible, educated, and successful children must rank as the most significant of anyone's personal accomplishments. With enormous credit to their mother, we can point to five such children. There is no higher calling or satisfaction than helping to create a loving family, providing for them, and setting children and grandchildren on their positive paths in life.

While I'm enthusiastically looking forward to many productive and happy years, most of my life already is behind me. My successes and failures and my decisions, both wise and foolish, are an unredeemable part of my past.

> As Omar Khayyam wrote in *The Rubaiyat*,
>
> The Moving Finger writes; and having writ, Moves on:
>
> Nor all your Piety nor Wit, Shall lure it back to cancel half a Line,
>
> Nor all your Tears wash out a Word of it.

But what about your life? What will you choose to do with it?

Answering that question, deciding what you believe—and what you do not—can be the compass for your entire life.

Starting with yourself at the core, what you believe in and value expands outward as a series of ever-widening concentric circles that encompass what you think about your purpose in life, God, human nature, family and friends, your country, even the planet.

We are taught both values and facts by those who love us. Quite properly, we consciously or subconsciously give great weight to what we learn from those we trust. The wisdom of those who came before us, especially the sages of the ages, deserve our respect and keen attention. Yet as we mature, we learn by listening, watching, reading, thinking, practicing, remembering, and experiencing life as we learn to decide for ourselves what we believe. By squarely facing the most fundamental questions, we choose our basic values, and those values essentially determine who and what we are.

* * *

I have always been sensitive about "wearing my religion on my sleeve." I am all too conscious of my many faults. In high school, I considered entering the ministry but quickly decided that I was not nearly good enough. Even though I've been everything from a Sunday-school teacher to a church trustee, I resolved when I entered public life not to talk publicly about my faith, feeling that using it for political gain would depreciate it.

Yet I know from my own experience that believing in God can give purpose and meaning to one's life. Christianity and virtually all other religions exist not only in holy books such as the Bible and Koran, but also in the very nature of the human soul. Whatever the fine points of theology, the fundamental precept of most religions teaches that God is love, and that as Jesus said, "Love thy neighbor as thyself."

But is there a basis for believing in God beyond the dogmatic assertions of theologians and people of faith whom you are expected to believe? Should you accept what others tell you to believe? The ultimate questions of life's meaning can be debated and explored.

I reached my own conclusions about God by looking at the world around me, the planets and the stars, and by studying the extraordinary complexity of living organisms. I observed the infinite order of physics, chemistry, and biology and recognized the precision of the universe. Could all this be true without the guiding hand of a Supreme Being—of God? I think not.

And I'm in good company. Sir Isaac Newton, who discovered the laws of gravity, the composition of light, and invented differential calculus, included in his *Principia Mathematica* his confession of faith: "The most beautiful system of the sun, planets, and comets could only proceed from...an intelligent and powerful being...the all-wise God perceives and understands all things."

James Wilson, a signer of both the Declaration of Independence and the U.S. Constitution and later a justice of the U.S. Supreme Court, believed that God's law was the "supreme" law of the land and the basis of moral obligations. He saw it as his moral duty to obey the will of God. "I can only say I *feel* that such is my duty. The law of nature and the law of revelation are both divine; they flow, though through different channels, from the same adorable source."

My faith also has been strengthened by reports on what are called near-death experiences. In his book *Life after Life,* Raymond Moody, a physician, documents a number of scientifically evaluated experiences of patients who appeared clinically dead—their EEG reading was a flat line, a legal definition of death. And yet, when they were resuscitated they accurately described what had occurred around them in the operating room. In one study of 116 patients conducted by a cardiologist, the men and women described

William Penn, the founder of Pennsylvania, wrote:

I expect to pass through life but once. If, therefore, there can be any kindness I can show, or any good things I can do to any fellow human being, let me do it now, and not defer or neglect it, as I shall not pass this way again.

If we try to follow his advice, we will feel good—and be doing something good in the process.

themselves floating above their body with a sense of perfect understanding as the doctors and nurses conversed, of peace and painlessness, of entering a tunnel composed of beautiful white light that radiated love and understanding. Virtually all of the people "who go through this experience come away believing that the most important thing in their life is love," Moody writes. "For them, the second most important thing in life is knowledge."

From this and other sources, I have come to believe that there is life after death.

I have also realized that prayer is a very important part of my life. I believe in praying as a way to keep grounded, even though I haven't been too keen on learning and repeating prayers written by others. Even the Lord's Prayer for me seems to have lost some of its deep meaning as I repeat it by rote. The intense emotional feeling it should engender has gotten dulled or even lost.

I prefer to create my own prayers, and recommend you try it. I pray every day, and suggest that you do, too.

Each evening when I crawl into bed, just before I go to sleep, I think: "Oh God, I give thanks for this wonderful day, for giving me my life, not once, but twice, and every day. Amen." (I am referring to my life being saved in an automobile accident in which my neck was broken. *I was wearing my seatbelt!*)

Striving to discern God's plan for us is a daily challenge—a lifetime challenge—but the effort gives life meaning.

Letting religious beliefs help guide our life is valuable even though we fall far short of the ideal. For example, we *know*, we feel the difference between right and wrong, but that doesn't mean we always follow our better instincts. Nor does it mean that we always can discern the differences in complex situations that have elements of both right and wrong.

If we do a good deed, if we help another person, if we are pleasant, if we are productive, we feel good. But if we refuse to be legitimately helpful, if we are surly, arrogant, or lazy, we feel bad.

Selfishness is also part of our human condition, and when self-interest clashes with our conscience, it's easy—sometimes too

Over the years I have developed my morning prayer which I say to myself, or out loud if I'm alone, during my morning run. Occasionally I've revised it. Here's my latest version:

Oh God, I give thanks for my many blessings,
For being alive, regaining my health, being a free man,
For being an American, living in these times;
For the abilities and opportunities you have given me,
For achieving my boyhood dream of becoming a United States congressman,
And for my new dreams of my books, Shuster Lodge, and Shuster enterprises,
For my family who came before, my mother and father, grandparents, aunts and uncles, cousins, relatives and ancestors, for my wife Patty, the mother of my children.
I give thanks for Peggy. Please be with Peggy.
I give thanks for Bobby and Megan. Please be with them.
I give thanks for Bill. Please be with Bill.
I give thanks for Ali and Garrett. Please be with them.
I give thanks for Emily and Greggie. Please be with them.
I give thanks for Bob. Please be with Bob.
I give thanks for Michael, Jonathan, and Daniel. Please be with them.
I give thanks for Gia. Please be with Gia.
I give thanks for Will, Andrew, and Jack. Please be with them.
I give thanks for my friends, supporters, and helpers.
Please help me to never let down my family or any of them.
You've known my prayer since the days of my youth, that my life be worthwhile in your Service.
Come into my heart, Oh God, take charge of me.
Give me the wisdom to know what is right and the strength to do what is right.
And in this wonderful time, let there be a re-birth of us all, starting with me.
Be with me, Oh God, this day, the only day of my life that's in the present.
Let it be a wonderful day in mind, spirit, and body, a day in which I have the strongest desire to achieve my day's plan, a day in which I give thanks for my many blessings.

Amen.

easy—to rationalize away that voice telling us what is right. Perhaps the most we can hope for in many circumstances is enlightened self-interest. That is, attempting to see not only what seems to be in our immediate self-interest, but rather what is best for us in the long run. By backing off and thinking about a particular situation, we sometimes can see that short-term gain actually produces long-term pain.

Love—in the broadest sense of the word, the Judeo-Christian sense of trying to love our neighbor—makes us feel good. Our willingness to sacrifice for others—for our family, our friends, for worthy causes—gives meaning to our lives. Hatred agitates us, often causes us to do things that actually can hurt us.

Aristotle wrote, "Man is a two-winged horse; one of noble and one of ignoble breed." Trying to harness the noble side of our human nature can be—in fact, should be—a life-long project. Listening to yourself, wrestling with your conscience isn't always easy, and often we fail. But trying turns us into better people than we otherwise might be.

If we are willing to believe in God and God's will despite the many unanswerable questions and mysteries of life, what else is worthy of our belief?

* * *

In these troubled times it is especially important to renew our faith in America. In 1983 I wrote my first book, *Believing in America*, from which I have occasionally included excerpts in this book. My thesis was that with all our country's imperfections, when compared with the rest of the world, America sparkles. The good so vastly outweighs the bad that America stands alone, preeminent, as a beacon of hope for the world. The intervening years have only reconfirmed it.

The drumbeat of negative news often obscures the extraordinary reality of America's progress: our life expectancy has increased from 47 to 77 years in one century; the average person's purchasing power has doubled in the past 40 years; the number of cars and miles driven has increased by 70 percent in the past 30 years, while air pollution has decreased by 30 percent and traffic fatalities by 20 percent.

The collapse of Communism, the rise of democracy and freedom in many countries, the economic strength of America, the flood of immigrants, legal and illegal, who see America as their promised land, all speak to the legitimacy of believing in America.

While the rise of terrorism, the increase of weapons of mass destruction in the hands of rogue states, and the hatred fomented against America by zealots and dictators conspire to make the world even more dangerous than it was during the Cold War, they make the preservation of our way of life, our freedom, and prosperity even more precious. Our willingness to go to war in Iraq in 2003 and the demonstration of America's military might in that conflict sends a clear message to the world: We are willing to defend freedom. Our generation reaffirms the motto of that early flag that flew in Westmoreland County, Pennsylvania, in 1775: "Don't tread on us."

Yet, there are those who see us as a great Satan, as capitalist exploiters, greedy materialists, as people who preach equality to the rest of the world but do not practice it at home. And there is more than a scintilla of truth in what they say. We are only human. We have made mistakes. Sometimes, grievous mistakes. From our very founding, our history of race relations has been a stain on our quest for equal opportunity for all. Yet, from a slave-holding nation that inconsistently claimed that "all men are created equal" through a bloody Civil War followed by a century of "Jim Crow" segregation laws and practices, America has made enormous progress, even though the dream remains imperfectly fulfilled.

Growing up in the Steel Valley during the 1940s, we participated in sports with black teammates, accepting them as full-fledged friends. Or, at least it seemed that way. Yet, racial epithets were a common part of our slang. And there always was an unspoken divide.

When our town's baseball team made it to the final rounds in Dayton, Ohio, an Alabama team refused to play us with a black athlete on our team. The coach put it to a team vote, and they voted to

Bud on his beloved palomino "Pitt" with the bicentennial
wagon train as it passed through Pennsylvania in 1976

play without Moe, our centerfielder. Moe said, "Go ahead, play. It's okay with me." (We lost.) Twenty years later, Moe was arrested robbing a bank in that same Ohio city, three hundred miles from his home. It doesn't take a psychologist to connect his crime with the searing impact of his rejection there so many years before.

In the Steel Valley of Western Pennsylvania, as in many communities across America, both color and ethnic lines were often brightly drawn. Back in the 1930s and '40s in Glassport, the blacks lived "up the hollow," the Italians, along the river, the Polish on "Polish Hill," and the "Americans" in the valley. We mixed in school or at work, but everyone always gravitated back to his or her "own kind."

Our Uncle Herman Strahl told us what it had been like to be a Jew in the early years of the twentieth century. As an eight-year-old, to escape the pogroms being inflicted on the Jews in Russia, he walked across Germany with his aunt to gain passage in steerage on a ship to America. Settling in the hill district of Pittsburgh, then the Jewish ghetto, he left school in the eighth grade to earn money for his family by selling newspapers. He had a prime corner on Grant Street, but had to defend it every Saturday, fighting off other boys who wanted his location. He went to night school to study accounting. Upon graduating, he hoped to apply for a job as an office boy at the P&LE Railroad, but they were not hiring Jews. At his teacher's suggestion, he changed his name from Strilkofsky to Strahl, applied for the job, and got it. Thirty years later, Uncle Herman was one of the top executives at the railroad. Only in America!

When I entered the Army straight after college and eventually became a counterintelligence agent, one of my assignments was to cover domestic intelligence, including the Middle Atlantic region of the Communist Party. The following year, 1955, a thirteen-year-old black boy named Emmett Louis Till was murdered in Mississippi for whistling at a white woman. Civil rights groups organized legitimate protest rallies around the country. It quickly became clear that the Communist Party was gearing up to foment hatred by infiltrating the rallies. My partner and I covered the Pittsburgh rally. More than three thousand people jammed into the Soldiers and Sailors Memorial Hall on a Sunday afternoon to call for justice.

Communists and Communist sympathizers marched outside carrying signs, agitating, while their counterparts inside shouted to inflame the crowd. A legitimate cause was being manipulated to divide the country. Sandpaper was being rubbed on an American sore.

The next day I mailed my check to join the NAACP, a decade before the civil rights movement caught fire. White Americans had to care, or the sting of radicals would poison the nation.

Looking back, it seems extraordinary that we had done so little for race relations nearly a century after the Civil War. As my good friend Congressman J. C. Watts likes to point out, we have come a long way since those days, but the dream of true equal opportunity still eludes us.

I regret to say that the civil rights movement lost me, along with many Americans, when the goals changed from equal rights for everyone to preferential rights for minorities. That's not what America stands for. And years of unfair treatment by past generations does not justify selecting certain classes of Americans in this generation for preferred treatment at the expense of other Americans. We need to work harder to provide *equal* opportunities for all.

It was my great privilege to play a key role in 1998 in electing J. C. Watts as the chairman of the Republican Conference in Congress, the first African American ever elected to Republican Congressional leadership. He was the best person for the job.

* * *

We Americans believe our freedoms are God-given. But people are not truly free if they don't have equal opportunity.

As we embrace our many freedoms, it is equally important that we embrace the responsibilities related to those freedoms.

If we believe in America, we are responsible for contributing to the well-being of our country.

If we believe in ourselves, we are responsible for determining how we are going to translate that belief into our daily actions.

If we believe in God, we are responsible for determining what God expects of us.

If we believe in our family, we are responsible for providing them with material, intellectual, and spiritual sustenance.

Deciding what we believe is the first step to putting us on our path for life. Think about it carefully, for you have only one life to live, and when you crawl into bed tonight, this day of your life will be gone forever.

Chapter Two
Achieving

Compared with what we ought to be, we are
only half awake...we make use of only a small
part of our mental and physical resources...
Better man owe their success to an extra
effort of will.

—William James

When my granddaughter Ali faxed me her straight-A report card, she wrote across the bottom, "I hope you're proud of me." Of course, I was. She had achieved something important. And she was proud of herself. She felt the wonderful satisfaction of accomplishing a goal.

Achieving a worthy goal makes life worthwhile. But Ali didn't achieve hers without effort. Sometimes we make the mistake of thinking we can realize a goal without putting forth the effort. That's not the way life works.

There is a certain kind of person I call the "Gonna-doer." "I'm gonna-do this, or I'm gonna-do that." I'm sure you know people like that. They're always bragging about what they are going to do but seldom actually follow through. I believe it's a good idea not to talk too much about what you intend to accomplish unless you're announcing it as a way to motivate yourself. Sometimes, for example, I tell a few friends what I am giving up for Lent as a way of stiffening my resolve. I would be embarrassed to fail.

But it's much more important to tell *yourself* what you are going to achieve. Really resolve deep down inside what you're going to accomplish, and then plan exactly how you're going to get there. Whether it's a long- or a short-term objective, developing the habit of setting goals will make them easier to achieve.

One of my heroes, Benjamin Franklin, wrote in his *Autobiography*, "Make your virtues daily habits and life will take care of itself." He made a list of the "virtues" to which he aspired, including resolution and industry. Franklin confessed that he often failed to practice his virtues but believed he was a better person for trying.

Ben Franklin made up a little book with a page for each week, listing what he considered to be virtues on the left and the days of the week across the top. He carried the book with him, and every evening, he gave himself black marks beside each fault he committed that day.

1. Temperance—Eat not to dullness; drink not to elevation.
2. Silence—Speak not but what may benefit others or yourself; avoid trifling conversation.
3. Order—Let all your things have their places; let each part of your business have its time.
4. Resolution—Resolve to perform what you ought; perform without fail what you resolve.
5. Frugality —Make no expense but to do good to others or yourself, i.e. waste nothing.
6. Industry—Lose no time; always be employ'd in something useful; cut off all unnecessary actions.
7. Sincerity—Use no hurtful deceit; think innocently and justly, and, if you speak, speak accordingly.
8. Justice—Wrong none by doing injuries, or omitting the benefits that are your duty.
9. Moderation—Avoid extremes; forbear resenting injuries so much as you think are your duty.
10. Cleanliness—Tolerate no uncleanliness in body, cloths or habitation.
11. Tranquility—Be not disturbed at trifles, or at accidents common or unavoidable.
12. Chastity—Rarely use venery but for health or offspring, never to dullness, weakness, or the injury of your own or another's peace or reputation.
13. Humility—Imitate Jesus and Socrates.

Most of us fall short of being the ideal person we'd like to be, but without trying we'd fall even shorter. Failure, in fact, can be a motivator. We can learn from our mistakes.

One evening many years ago, I was at our Republican members Chowder & Marching Club get-together at a fellow congressman's Capitol Hill townhouse. Fellow C&M member Richard Nixon was reminiscing about his life in politics. He told us that losing an election destroys some men (or women), while others learn from the defeat. They strengthen their resolve to try again or refocus their energies on other goals. He would know. He picked himself up from a crushing presidential run against John F. Kennedy in 1960 and a failed California gubernatorial race against Pat Brown in 1963. Later, after Watergate, he rehabilitated his reputation to become a respected elder statesman. Former House Speaker Newt Gingrich lost his first two elections to Congress. Even Abraham Lincoln lost a number of elections, including two Senate races, before winning the presidency.

When I lost my race for whip, the second-ranking office among House Republicans, by three votes in the Republican Conference in 1980, one of my supporters came over to console me. I shook his hand, smiled, waved my fist high in the air, and announced, "Tomorrow I start writing my book!" Losing that election, especially by such a close margin, really hurt. But instead of concentrating on my disappointment, I refocused my energy on a new, positive endeavor. I immersed myself in writing my first book, *Believing in America*. Looking back, I think I'm more proud of the way I handled myself in defeat than in some of my victories.

Writing *Believing in America* was a major undertaking. I needed to learn more about the craft of writing, so I took a creative writing course at night. Along with my congressional duties, I had to discipline myself to get organized and to manage each hour of the day, including weekends, for more than a year. But I was reminded once again that the satisfaction of achieving a complicated, lengthy project far outweighs the sacrifice.

It's important to recognize that discipline is not a dirty word. Too often, we think of it as something cold and hard, of being forced to do something we don't want to do. It's the castor oil of life—sometimes required, but never desired. Discipline, in the best sense of the word, is not being ordered to do something by your parents or teacher or boss. It's deciding what you want to do and then figuring out how. Discipline is one of the forces behind achievement, and the thrill of achieving ranks among life's sweetest satisfactions.

Growing up in Glassport, Pennsylvania, during the Great Depression and World War II, I saw many wonderful examples of young people who succeeded in spite of the hard times and seemingly limited opportunities. Velma Backstrom was a high-school classmate of mine, who, like most of us, came from a family of very limited means. To make matters worse, she became gravely ill, missed much of a school year, and had to repeat a grade. (Before her illness, I confess that she wrote some of my papers for my eighth-grade health class.) She was indefatigable. When she graduated a year behind us, she won a scholarship to Pitt, worked part-time to cover her expenses, and finished college with honors. While teaching school, she continued her education at night and became Dr. Velma Backstrom Saire, a highly respected assistant school superintendent and adjunct professor at Carnegie Mellon University.

I knew others like Velma who came out of our little mill town and made something of themselves. They achieved worthy goals because they dedicated and disciplined themselves. They found the motivation, the energy, to exert an extra effort of will. I admire each of them.

Unfortunately, there also are examples of young people who had wonderful opportunities but threw them away. Lou Kusserow was one of my boyhood idols. He was a great athlete, smart, handsome, and from a loving family just a few blocks from our home. As a little kid, I would stand in the alley behind our house waiting for the football players to trudge back from their practice field to the high school so I could tag along with Lou. He went off on an athletic scholarship to Columbia University—the Ivy League—where he became an all-American running back and then on to the New York Giants, where he had a fine career. Lou was our hometown hero. After pro-football, he was hired by NBC Sports as a producer. For several years his name appeared among the credits at the end of NBC's nationally televised sporting events. I know the story because I was working at RCA, NBC's parent company, at the time.

Lou developed a drinking problem that got so bad that they sent him away to get sober. He returned, got his job back, but soon relapsed. After a few more tries, NBC finally fired him. Years later, at Glassport's 50th Anniversary Varsity Sports Banquet, where I had the privilege of being the speaker, I learned that Lou was a greeter at a bar in Palm Springs. One of his successful high-school teammates told me he had called Lou to urge him to come to the banquet because he would be an honored guest. Lou replied that he would come if someone would send him an airplane ticket, because he couldn't afford one. Too embarrassed by the conversation, his old teammate thought it best not to send the ticket.

My other high-school hero joined the Marine Corps. Upon discharge, he went to work in the mill, played semi-pro football, became an alcoholic, and eventually deserted his wife and children. Many years later, I helped get him into the state veterans home.

How could this be? How could my high-school heroes, the town's heroes, turn out like this? They had everything: brains, looks, extraordinary athletic ability, opportunity. Yet, their lives were failures, and they badly hurt their families.

The truth is, they didn't have everything. They had almost everything. In fact, they had almost everything in greater abundance than most young people. But they lacked one crucial ingredient. They lacked the discipline to keep their problem under control. They didn't manage themselves. They didn't motivate themselves to achieve worthy goals following their athletic careers.

As a sixteen-year-old, my top priority was to get my own car. I had to earn the money to buy my dreamboat, so I walked the main street of nearby McKeesport, going from store to store, looking for a job. Finally, I found one as a stock boy at Samuels shoe store.

Once I had saved $175, I bought my first chariot—a beat-up 1938 Studebaker. I had to take the battery out each night and set it beside our coal furnace warming it so the car would start in the morning. The engine had "soft-plugs" in its sides that periodically popped out, causing the water to spill on the road and overheat the engine. So I had to carry extra plugs, a small hammer, and jugs of water to make emergency roadside repairs. I budgeted $1 a week for gas at 25 cents a gallon, and I would have gone without food, if necessary, to keep that old jalopy running. Taking that first step— setting my goal to get my car—gave me the discipline required to make it come true. Discipline, then, is the father of achievement, without which desires can never be turned into realities.

It was my privilege to work closely with many outstanding men and women in Congress. Invariably, the ones I saw achieve the most were well organized and self-disciplined. Unlike my failed high-school heroes, several built upon their athletic fame to achieve other successes. Jim Bunning, the Hall of Fame pitcher, who was elected to both the House and Senate, is one of the most serious-minded and capable men with whom I served. Congressman Jim Ryun and Senator Ben Nighthorse Campbell, two Olympic champions, could be seen regularly working out in the House gym. Bill Bradley, the Princeton all-American and Knicks basketball star, was one of the most highly respected members of the Senate. Most congressional leaders with whom I served practiced enormous self-discipline. I recall jogging early one morning on Nob Hill in San Francisco and bumping into Dick Gephardt, the Democratic leader of the House, who was chugging along in the gray light of early dawn.

Members of Congress, like most successful people, have enormous demands on them. Occasionally, while waiting for votes in the back of the chamber, a member would complain, "My staff is running me ragged. They have me scheduled solidly from Friday night through Sunday this weekend." I would nod and mumble something like, "Yeah, there aren't enough hours in the day." But what I thought was, "Why the hell are you letting your staff set your schedule? You should be making those decisions."

The point is that deciding what not to do with your time is every bit as important as deciding what to do. On Friday nights when our boys were playing high-school football and our girls were marching in the band, my staff knew better than even to suggest another commitment for me. And Sundays were for family. Period! Some of my greatest joys included helping my grandson Bobby buy his first not-so-new car, and cheering for my granddaughter Megan as she marched with her baton group, the Twirling Kittens. Juggling my schedule to attend "grandparents day" with my granddaughter Emily, or rooting for my grandson Garrett at his baseball games is simply a matter of keeping my priorities straight.

There's nothing wrong with being brutal about your time, because that's how you get more things done. I discovered that lesson during college. From six in the morning until eleven at night, I made every hour count: classes, studying, debate team, YMCA, Sigma Chi, Inter-fraternity Council, honorary societies, working on Saturdays at Samuels shoe store, and even some purposeful "hanging out" in the students' Tuck Shop.

As management guru Peter Drucker emphasizes in his books, concentration is one of the keys to most results in life. When I got to Congress, I was appointed to both the Transportation and Education Committees. I made three fundamental decisions that greatly influenced my entire career. First, I decided that because there were so many different, complicated national issues and so many demands on me as a congressman, I would concentrate on developing expertise in one area. Second, I decided that improving transportation in my Central Pennsylvania congressional district would help create much-needed jobs and modernize the region. Third, I knew I did not want to spend my congressional career being against everything. I wanted to be a builder, and while a fiscal conservative, I could in good conscience support spending tax dollars to improve transportation, flood control, clean water systems, and industrial parks—investing to benefit people long after the tax dollars had been spent. So I focused my time and energy on the Transportation Committee. I like to think I was the best freshman member on the committee, but the corollary is that I probably was the worst on the Education Committee.

Many members divided their time between two or even three committees, often running back and forth to catch parts of hearings taking place simultaneously. It's not for me to criticize that approach. They probably developed a broader understanding of more issues than I. But concentrating on developing my expertise in one field was the right approach for me. And it paid off years later when I became chairman of the committee. I had a thorough understanding of the areas over which we had jurisdiction.

Eventually, after I had developed my transportation knowledge, I branched out. My election as chairman of the Republican Policy Committee exposed me to virtually every major issue coming before the Congress. When I was appointed to the Select Intelligence Committee, eventually becoming its ranking member, I was able to build on my experience as a former counterintelligence agent to contribute in the field of national security. But even as I broadened my experience over the years, I was always sensitive about not spreading myself too thin, about expending my energy wisely.

By recognizing where our talents lie, we can allocate our efforts accordingly. It can be hard to face up to our limitations, but if we don't, we may be setting ourselves up to fail. It is crucial to choose a career where you have a reasonable chance for success based on your own abilities and efforts, for that choice will determine in large measure how you spend your life.

Looking back, I'm lucky that I wasn't a better pianist. Growing up in a musical family has always made music an enjoyable part of my life. I started taking piano lessons at age five from my cousin Sylvia. On Saturday afternoons I had to sit silently beside my father listening to the New York Metropolitan Opera on the radio. I performed in high-school concerts, played in a dance band, and performed with the Altoona, Pennsylvania, symphony. Had I been better, I might have majored in music and played the piano professionally in a band or a cocktail lounge. But it would not have made for a very productive or pleasant life because I was not good enough to make the big time. So it is with many career paths.

In any job, there are factors beyond our control that may help us succeed or cause us to fail, no matter what we do. As a trustee at the University of Pittsburgh during the late 1960s when student

Bud rehearses for his performance with the Altoona Symphony

riots over the Vietnam War were roiling the country, I concluded that being a president of a university in that tumultuous environment, coupled with the problem of satisfying the conflicting demands of the faculty, alumni, the government, and the board of trustees, made the job impossible.

Conversely, seizing opportunities when they appear can contribute to your success. As Shakespeare wrote, "We must take the current when it serves, or lose our ventures." That means being flexible enough to change course if an unexpected opportunity appears. During World War II, one of General Dwight D. Eisenhower's guiding principles was to always plan ahead but be prepared to change your plans. That is good advice.

But there are also times when you have to stick to your guns.

When I was RCA's district manager in Pittsburgh, an opening occurred for the no. 2 job in government marketing in Washington. After sleeping on it and discussing it with my family, I talked to the vice president who had hired me about my interest in the job. It must have been my boyhood dream of becoming a congressman that drew me to Washington.

Three years later, after I was transferred to the new job, RCA's computer division vice president of government marketing died suddenly, and, after some interim changes, I was asked to replace him. But I was told I would not be made a vice president because I was "too young."

Again, after sleeping on it, I made a gutsy, possibly foolhardy, decision based on principle. I said, "Thanks, but if I don't deserve the title, I don't deserve the job. I'll just stay in the no. 2 spot until you find a new vice president." I had received good performance reviews for the previous three years and I knew I could do the work. I also knew that there was no one else in the division who had the experience. I had some leverage. Within a month, RCA's board of directors elected me a vice president. Looking back, I'm a bit surprised at my "chutzpah," but the lesson is that sometimes we need to take a risk to achieve an opportunity. We need to stand firm on principle.

But we also need to understand our limitations. I thought being a vice president of RCA's computer division meant I knew how to run a business, but I was in for a big surprise when I became president of Datel, a new, unprofitable computer terminal company. I suddenly realized that an executive of a big company must be an expert in a very narrow part of the business, whereas my new job required me to be skilled in general management, in which I had no experience. Fortunately, however, I had my MBA and PhD in business to fall back on. I then made some risky decisions based on principles I had learned because I didn't have broad management experience.

Our sales were poor and our product was unreliable. The terminals were priced so low that the business wouldn't be profitable even if sales went up. So I shut down the plant, told the engineers they had to significantly improve reliability, and, to their disbelief, informed the sales force that we were increasing the price by 30 percent. I wasn't at all sure I was making the right decisions. I had a knot in my stomach for several weeks. But I knew we never would be successful if we kept producing an unreliable product at an unprofitable price.

I also put together an excellent management team, although I made at least one very bad decision. My controller worked long hours and tried hard, but he wasn't cutting it and I had to let him go. I felt terrible because I had hired him away from UNIVAC, where we had worked together. Plus, he was a friend. But if we didn't get control of the business, there wouldn't be any business. I know it was the right decision, but it wasn't easy. Sometimes in life we have to make very distasteful decisions. But if we don't make them, we will be inflicting greater damage on ourselves and others who depend on us.

My decision to run for Congress was another risky venture. After selling Datel in 1971, I was free and financially secure. One morning I opened the *Washington Post* and read that the 1972 reapportionment had created a new Pennsylvania congressional district that included Bedford County, where our farm was located. The opportunity captured my imagination. The timing was right. I could afford to put some money into financing a campaign. And if I lost, I was confident I could find another job. In fact, I violated an important principle when I decided to run for Congress—"the wing-walker's rule: Never let go of what you have until you have a hold of something else." But I saw it as a chance of a lifetime and worth the risk.

Finally, I decided to test the water, visiting several Republican households and sending letters to others. We then polled those homes as well as others we had not contacted. When I saw the results from the homes I had visited, I said, "Damn, I can win this race!"—though almost nobody believed me.

I went with the family to Puerto Rico for ten days, sat in the sun, and wrote a three-volume campaign plan based on my experience that was really a marketing plan. I was the product, and we were aiming at a one-day sale. Looking back, we had some good laughs over my political naivete, but it was a start.

We came back from vacation, I announced my candidacy, and assembled a campaign team of my family, several people from Datel, and some fraternity brothers from college. Out of 500,000 people in the 9th Congressional District, virtually nobody knew who I was. Nor

Bobby, Gia, Debbie, Billy, Peggy, Patty, and Bud during the first campaign in 1972

did the politicians take me seriously. My opponent made the fatal mistake of assuming he could coast into Congress without conducting a vigorous campaign. After a fraternity brother painted an old school bus red-white-and-blue and hooked up a loudspeaker to play marching music, we drove through communities stopping to knock on Republican doors. Each day was meticulously planned the day before by an "advance man" who had mapped out the streets and identified the Republican homes. My wife, Patty, went down one side of the street while I canvassed the other, each of us with two advance people, knocking on doors and leaving brochures if no one was home. The mother and sister of Ann Eppard, my Datel executive assistant who became my chief of staff, volunteered to do nightly polling of the homes to measure our performance. We hired an extremely capable political consultant to do our TV, radio, and newspaper advertising, as well as direct mailers and opposition research. The primary campaign cost me $117,000 out of my own pocket. I couldn't expect many people to contribute to a political novice whom nobody knew. But after we won the primary with an eight-point margin, we realized that although we had struggled through a steep learning curve, we had a winning formula. Still, it took a tremendous team effort over the years to win the Republican nomination fifteen times and the Democratic nomination nine times (on a write-in ballot), a feat never before achieved in Pennsylvania's history. (Bragging isn't polite, but a lot of people deserve to share the credit for this accomplishment.) And our future campaigns would have faltered had I not performed in office.

The point of the story is that you can achieve wonderful goals in life if—and this is a big IF—you are willing to throw yourself into it heart and soul, discipline yourself to plan and organize, and work to achieve your goals. Nor can the importance of having your family and friends behind you be overstated.

Even though achieving some goals requires tremendous effort and concentration, you don't have to be in pain to be productive. Today, with cell phones, E-mail, and faxes, you don't have to limit productivity to an office. I've taken part in many important conference

Bud, Patty, and the kids celebrate the first election victory

calls on my cell phone while sitting around the swimming pool or at the farm. Personal productivity can be greatly increased by organizing yourself to do what I call "two-fers": reading while listening to the news; exercising while thinking through your day's plan; scheduling business meetings around meals. "Let's walk and talk" is standard procedure for members of Congress going from their office to vote in the Capitol.

Even little gimmicks can help make your day more pleasant and productive. After doing my crunches for several years as part of my daily workout, it occurred to me that instead of simply counting to a hundred I could count in German. Once I got into the habit, my mind wandered to memories of my many trips to Germany—I relived my visits to Herbitzheim from where some of our ancestors emigrated in 1749; to Berlin and through Checkpoint Charlie into what was then Communist East Berlin; to Heidelberg where, following the student tradition, I carved my initials in a table at the *Bierstube*; and to the Black Forest, where we were guests of a count in his castle. When I do my back exercises, instead of counting numerically, I count mnemonically (a system using code words and related visual associations to improve memory). These are just little things, but they help rekindle fond memories and add pleasure to my day.

Another self-motivating trick I use when I think I'm too tired to do something I know I should do is to tell myself, "I'm just too lazy." If you're like me, you'll find yourself thinking, "No, I'm not!"

Sometimes little tasks don't seem worthwhile, and yet they can be building blocks for greater things. In ancient Greece, when the Spartans conquered Athens, they captured Epaminondas, one of the most highly revered Athenian generals. They thought they could break the spirit of the Athenians by making their beloved general look foolish, so they took him up on a platform in front of the people and appointed him the new garbage collector of Athens. Epaminondas stepped forward and announced to the applause of the citizens, "If the job does not confer its dignity on me, I shall confer my dignity upon the job." Giving a task your best shot usually pays off, no matter how trivial or even demeaning it may seem.

When I went to work at Samuels shoe store as a sixteen-year-old stock boy, earning $2.50 each Saturday working from nine in the morning until nine at night, I was determined to become a salesman. The only reason I got the job was because my older cousin Dorothy had worked there before becoming a buyer at a major department store. Mr. Samuels said she was the best sales person he ever had. I guess my competitive juices whispered: "I can be as good as she was." I learned that Mr. Samuels came to work a few minutes before nine on Saturdays, so I always got there by 8:30 to sweep the steps and wash the front window. After closing time, I stayed to break down and bundle up empty shoeboxes. When the salesmen were busy with other customers, I stood at the door to catch the next prospect, lead him to an empty chair, and quickly get one of his shoes off (so he couldn't walk out), and begin my sales pitch. After the first month, Mr. Samuels made me a salesman. I ended up working on Saturdays for the next seven years, finally earning $25 a day (equal to over $200 today).

I never was as good as Dorothy, but I like to think that I came close.

Chapter Three

Persuading

You can catch more flies with honey than with vinegar.
--A. Lincoln

One evening when my cousin Dorothy explained the importance of being able to persuade people to your point of view, she looked me squarely in the eye and yawned. In a few moments, I yawned. "See," she exclaimed, smiling. "That's the power of suggestion!" (I just yawned as I write this.)

My grandson Will, at the age of five, unconsciously developed a habit of asking, "Right?" after telling us something. I think he's on the way to becoming a professional persuader.

Our success in life depends in large measure on our ability to communicate, and communication takes different forms in different situations. People often think the art of persuasion is limited to salesmanship, courtroom theatrics, or advertising, but it is a fundamental component of how we relate to all of the people in our lives. Every time you walk into a room, you hope to convince the people you meet that you are a good person, that they should like you. I try to greet people enthusiastically. Positive energy is infectious. It's like giving someone a shot of adrenalin. And if you want to be a persuader, it's helpful to associate yourself with positive, emotional symbols: your country, your school, your community. You also hope to win them over to your views: The second war in Iraq was justified, or

Barry Bonds is washed up. And sometimes, you want to talk them into taking a specific action: Don't wear that blue dress; vote for my candidate; loan me the car Saturday night; let's move to the suburbs.

But what are the elements of persuasion? How can you get others to buy what you have to say?

When I decided to run for Congress, I met with Eddie Mahe, a professional political consultant, to get his guidance. I laid out in great detail the issues that I thought were important to the 9th District of Pennsylvania and the nation. I explained what my positions would be. I identified the key organizations that I thought would support me based on my political philosophy. He held up his hands and said, "Wait a minute! That's all just fine, but first you've got to get the people to like you."

He was right. If people don't like you, if they're not comfortable with you, they're not going to be persuaded by what you say, even if you have a ton of facts on your side. The word *persuasion* comes from the Latin, *per suasionem,* which means "by sweetness."

Congresswoman Bella Abzug was a case in point. She was one of the smartest, hardest working, and most knowledgeable members of Congress with whom I served. But Bella was not effective in getting her legislation through the House. There was a saying that when she went to the floor with an issue, she had fifty votes against her before she opened her mouth—and from both sides of the aisle. Why? Because Bella was angry, militant, and disrespectful of her colleagues. When Speaker Carl Albert told her she had to remove her trademark broad-brimmed hat, she replied with an epithet. So instead, the sergeant at arms removed her from the chamber. She failed to achieve her goals because she was abrasive.

Conversely, one day I noticed Congressman Danny Rostenkowski, the then powerful chairman of the Ways and Means Committee, walking through the Capitol. He was immersed in very serious legal difficulties that ultimately led to time in jail (although he was later pardoned). But as people passed him, he would nod pleasantly and smile. He made them feel good. I think he made himself feel good as well.

General Colin Powell said, "Perpetual optimism is a force multiplier." A positive attitude energizes and motivates people. A negative attitude destroys the incentive to achieve and perform.

Although Congressman Henry Hyde has been involved in some extremely controversial issues—he was chairman of the committee that brought the impeachment charges against President Bill Clinton, and he is an outspoken leader in the Right To Life movement—he is well liked. Henry is pleasant, courteous, and a great raconteur. His wife once told me, "Henry *thinks* funny." Telling stories is a wonderful way to put people at ease and get them smiling or laughing with you. It's an ability worth cultivating. Although one has to be careful about telling locker room jokes, members of Congress often get each other chuckling with stories as they relax in the back of the chamber waiting for votes. Obviously, stories that embarrass another person should not be told.

Telling a story on yourself is both the best and safest kind. I've got a lot of mileage out of my "mustard" story, which really happened. I was at a Rotary luncheon, where my mind was on my upcoming speech as I spread some "mustard" on my sandwich. I ate my sandwich, which tasted fine. Then I noticed everyone had a cup of "mustard" in front of their plates, and after eating their sandwiches, they all ate their "mustard." Something wasn't quite right, so I dipped my finger in my "mustard" cup and tasted it. It was butterscotch pudding. Bad enough that I had plastered it on my sandwich, but what a blockhead I was to eat it without even noticing! It's the kind of story that gets a good laugh and suggests that you're probably an okay guy if you can spoof yourself.

I recommend opening speeches with a humorous story. It relaxes the audience and makes them more receptive to your persuasion. And it's important to carefully think through what you're going to say, whether it's a formal speech, informal presentation, or simply a conversation where you hope to win someone over to your views. President Franklin Roosevelt was one of the great persuaders of the twentieth century. He came across in his fireside chats as warm, relaxed, confident, even spontaneous. But when an historian was going through the archives, he came across twenty different drafts of a single fireside chat, with extensive revisions in FDR's handwriting. The great, supposedly extemporaneous, persuader had paid meticulous attention to every word and phrase in his talks.

Still, preparation isn't all there is to persuasion. The first-ever televised presidential debate, between John F. Kennedy and Richard Nixon, is instructive, but not because of the candidates' policy differences. Both were polished speakers. The polls indicated that JFK won the televised debate, but Nixon won the radio debate. How could that be? It was the same debate. Analysis showed that people liked the way Kennedy looked—tan, handsome, smiling, relaxed—while Nixon had what came to be called his "five o'clock shadow." He had shaved that morning, but not again before the evening debate. He had also resisted wearing make-up, so he projected a pale image. Based on what people *heard*, Nixon won the debate logically by pounding home his well-organized arguments. But based on what people *saw*, Kennedy won the debate emotionally, and television was seen by several million more people. Emotion trumped logic.

There's an old saying, "You never have a second chance to make a good first impression." Nixon's five o'clock shadow is a reminder that appearance counts. While clothes don't make the man (or woman), nobody is attracted to a slob. There's no substitute for neatness—spiffy grooming, polished shoes, and, for a woman, attractive make-up. And physical fitness radiates vitality. Likewise, the first few words out of your mouth indicate that you're an assured, friendly, articulate person, or a hesitant mumbler who doesn't know good English.

Jack Hazzard, the man who hired me at UNIVAC after I completed my military duty, was one of the best sales executives I've ever known, routinely selling million dollar computers to corporate CEOs over stiff IBM competition. Though he walked with a bad limp from childhood polio, he exuded positive energy and looked sharp. He also had one other trait. Like my cousin Dorothy, he understood the power of suggestion in getting others to agree with you. He wouldn't even ask, "How are you today?" without nodding his head

Bud demonstrates a UNIVAC computer system

Lt. Bud Shuster, Infantry/ Military Intelligence, at Fort McHenry, Maryland, 1954

Bud on guard duty at Fort Riley, Kansas

affirmatively and smiling. You unconsciously found yourself smiling, nodding your head affirmatively, and replying, "Just great." Getting people in a positive frame of mind, getting them to agree about little things, is a starting point toward bigger agreements.

But even if you've used all the available tools to establish good rapport, you still won't be very persuasive if your focus is on what *you* want, instead of what your listener wants. I've received hundreds of letters over the years that start out, "I want...I believe...I can...I...I...I..."

Professor Robert Oliver wrote in *The Psychology of Persuasive Speech* that people act on what they believe to be in their self-interest. They can be appealed to emotionally, logically, or even through rationalization. We make a huge mistake thinking people will do something because *we* want them to.

Recently, I had a sophisticated client who prepared a detailed letter to be presented to a government agency stating the reasons why that agency should select their product. When they sent it to me for review, the draft document read like a legal brief full of technical language. I said, "Hold it, fellas. These are all very important points, but don't we want to put the sizzle up front? Why not start the letter by telling them how the product will make *their* operation better?" The light went on for these financial and technical wizards. They were pros in their fields, but they were kindergarteners in the world of persuasion.

The first major crisis in my fledgling computer career occurred when U.S. Steel threatened to cancel all the UNIVAC orders I had secured as UNIVAC's national account manager to U.S. Steel. Although IBM had been their exclusive computer supplier, U.S. Steel's computer brass had been sold largely by the software research work being done by Dr. Grace Murray Hopper in our computer lab to develop an English-language programming system that would replace the slower, more costly machine coding. Grace already was famous as the Naval Officer in World War II who had helped break "Purple," the Japanese code that led us to a great naval victory in the South Pacific. We brought Grace to Pittsburgh to meet with U.S. Steel and, after many meetings, they agreed to order several multi-million dollar large-scale UNIVAC systems based on our commitment to provide the software. Grace was given a large team of our best programmers, a substantial budget, and a timetable to develop what eventually came to be called COBOL—Common Business-Oriented Language.

Cracking U.S. Steel made me a star in the company, even though it was Grace's genius that had created the opportunity. We worked closely for several months back-and-forth between U.S. Steel's computer people in Pittsburgh and Grace's lab in Philadelphia. And when our COBOL development team began missing benchmark deadlines, more programmers were added and her budget was increased.

Finally, one day, I was summoned to UNIVAC headquarters in New York. When I got there, I was taken behind closed doors with the senior vice president who informed me, "We've decided to pull the plug on this COBOL research project. It's way behind schedule and over budget. You go tell U.S. Steel we don't think we can get it beyond the research stage. We'll let Grace have a few programmers to play with it, and maybe someday we'll have a software product that works. In the meantime, tell them we'll give them a dozen more programmers to help them get the machine coding completed for their accounting system."

I squirmed in my chair for a few minutes trying to explain how unhappy U.S. Steel would be, but he dismissed me.

As I got on the elevator on the 23rd floor and pushed the down button, I saw my shining star turning to dust. The company wasn't going to accept our decision. We would be kicked out, IBM would have a lock on U.S. Steel forever, and I would be a dismal failure.

But as I got off the elevator on the first floor, I remembered that Mr. VanGorder, U.S. Steel's top computer honcho, had previously worked at IBM with Mr. Bibby, our new UNIVAC president. I took a deep breath, mumbled "shit," got back on the elevator, and pushed the button for the 24th floor, Mr. Bibby's office. What did I have to lose? I was finished if I lost U.S. Steel.

Fortunately, Mr. Bibby was in his office and agreed to see me. I explained the situation to him, emphasizing that not only would our name be "mud" in Pittsburgh, we would be tarred with a bad reputation throughout the industry. UNIVAC would never crack IBM's stranglehold. UNIVAC would be a failure, and although I certainly didn't say the words, it obviously meant that he, the new president of UNIVAC, would be a failure too.

"You think Grace can pull this off?" he asked.

"Absolutely!" I replied, trying to sound confident.

He pushed his buzzer and told his secretary to get VanGorder on the phone. After a long, friendly, but animated conversation, he finally said, "Okay, Van, damn't, we'll do it! But my future's riding on this. I know...I know. Yours is too. I won't let you down."

After he hung up, he stared at me, "Boy, I hope you know what you're doing."

"Yes, sir. Thank you, sir," I replied, and got out of the building as fast as I could, before the executives on the floor below could get their hands on me.

As they say, the rest is history. COBOL finally worked, and eventually became the industry standard. I'm convinced Mr. Bibby was persuaded because he could envision himself getting scalped. His future was riding on the success of COBOL. (Years later, it was my privilege to support congressional action to promote Grace to the rank of Commodore in the Navy reserve. It was a title that had not been used since the promotion of Commodore Oliver Hazard Perry for winning the Battle Lake Erie in 1812.)

We all like to think that we act rationally, that we make decisions based on sound reasoning, evidence and solid facts. And, of course, people do make many decisions that way, so it's important to learn how to think logically and how to use logic in persuading others. I'm convinced that my experience on the Pitt debate team helped teach me how to think logically, how to analyze a set of facts or opinions and marshal them to bolster my argument.

My Pitt debate coach, Dr. Robert "Rocky" Newman, wrote a book titled *Evidence*. He emphasized the importance of critically evaluating information, of testing it: Is it consistent with our own knowledge and experience? How credible is the source? Does the source have a past record of accuracy? Is it biased? Does it reflect expertise?

People use two kinds of reasoning, often unconsciously. Deductive reasoning is based on self-evident propositions. If A=B and A=C, then B=C. Inductive reasoning is based on observation and experience. If I know the sun has come up every morning in the past, I induce that it will come up tomorrow morning. You can be more persuasive if you include both types of reasoning in making your case, being very careful not to exaggerate.

Ben Franklin said, "So convenient a thing it is to be a reasonable creature, since it enables one to find or make a reason for everything one has a mind to do." It's human nature to rationalize, to find reasons or excuses to justify our actions. And the more educated or sophisticated a person is, the more apt he is to invent "reasons" for doing what he wants to do. I recently "reasoned" that I needed a nifty new power drill I saw on display at the hardware store. I laughed at my rationalization, but bought it anyway.

It's important to understand rationalization, not only because it helps us evaluate our own decisions, but also because it is a powerful motivator in persuading others: Buy that car, you deserve it; come with me to the movies, it's educational; let's eat that cake, there aren't that many calories in it.

Nor is rationalization necessarily bad. It can help us feel better. It can salve emotional wounds. When someone we care about dies after a long illness, we say, "It's for the best." When our team does poorly, we say, "Wait until next year." It can help us see the bright side of a bad situation to regain a positive outlook.

We also need to be aware of subliminal persuasion, a technique used by advertising to subconsciously motivate us to believe something or take a specific action. Wilson Key, in his book, *Subliminal Seduction*, described how some movie theaters flashed high-speed messages that were invisible to the conscious mind on screens: "Hungry? Eat popcorn," and "Drink Coca-Cola." During a six-week test, popcorn sales increased 57 percent and Coke sales 18 percent. It's part of America, but it helps to remember that we're being bombarded by subtle, sometimes subliminal, emotional messages.

It's important to evaluate information you read or hear to see if it makes sense or is simply a rationalization or emotional appeal. At the Army Counterintelligence School, we were taught how to turn raw information into intelligence by determining if our source had been reliable in the past and then measuring the validity of the information against independently gathered facts.

Responsible journalists use a similar methodology in gathering information for a story. Much of the information we receive is only partially accurate at best. That doesn't mean we shouldn't listen carefully to what we're told. As Ronald Reagan said about the Soviet Union, "Trust, but verify!"

Remember, others are constantly, albeit often subconsciously, evaluating what you say, judging how reliable your opinions have been in the past, and how your views stack up against their own knowledge and experience. Day by day, year by year, people are learning to trust your judgment. They are inclined to be persuaded by you if you have built up a reservoir of trust.

Nothing is quite so deflating as telling someone a "fact," only to have them produce solid evidence that proves it's wrong. In the early days of the airbag, consumer watchdog Ralph Nader testified before our committee that the safety device reliably inflated in serious crashes. We produced a report from the National Highway Traffic Safety Administration showing that the airbag failed to inflate in 43 percent of "tow-away" crashes. When I debated him on national television, instead of responding to the evidence, he attacked me personally: "You're the kind of person who would sell thalidomide to a pregnant woman!" he sneered. This wild accusation was the high point of the debate for me because it destroyed his credibility. He actually helped make my position more persuasive.

A few months later, a *Washington Post* reporter told me, "Nader used to get a lot of ink, but we don't pay too much attention to him anymore because he comes across as a fanatic." People aren't going to pay much attention to you if what you say isn't credible.

As much as we might like to win someone over, it's important to remember the difference between facts and opinions. Years ago, I was having dinner with a group of doctoral students, discussing economics with our dissertation advisor, Dr. Photias. I made a comment, "Well, the truth is..." when he stopped me. "According to whom?" he asked. Often the "truth" looks quite different, depending on your perspective. Military men say not enough money is being spent on defense, while social workers say the same about social services. The real truth is that both are opinions. The dollars in the budget are facts. And people are entitled to different opinions, but not to different facts. Nader was entitled to his opinion that the government should require airbags in all cars but not to his assertion that they were reliable. Eventually, they did become more reliable, and they can save lives. But they have never measured up to their proponents' initial claims. The facts could not sway Nader because he was emotionally committed to his position. My purpose, of course, was not to persuade him, but rather to persuade the television audience and, ultimately, my colleagues in Congress.

Nevertheless, if you must disagree with someone, it's important not to make it personal. In public life, disputes often can be handled professionally and unemotionally, but in personal relationships, it's more difficult. Feelings can be hurt. Sometimes relationships can be destroyed.

I learned that the hard way on a college debate trip. I had agreed to drive some of the team in my car to Allegheny College with the proviso that we leave immediately after the tournament so I could get to my job waiting tables on time. After the tournament, I agreed to briefly drop by the reception at the student union honoring the debaters. As time passed, I kept urging my teammates to leave, to no avail. Finally, exasperated, I walked into the center of the group, pointed my finger at them, and said in a loud, angry voice: "All right. To hell with all of you! I'm leaving without you!" and I stormed out of the building. I did wait a few minutes in the car, they showed up, and we sped back to Pittsburgh in frosty silence.

The next week, Rocky called me in and asked, "Are you proud of the way you acted last Saturday afternoon?" Still angry, I tried to explain that I had clearly told everyone before the trip that I had to leave promptly for my job. He nodded, folded his hands, and furrowed his brow at me. "Well," he said, "you were one hundred percent right, and the way you went about it was one hundred percent wrong. Do you think shouting at us in front of a large group of people helped?"

"I wasn't shouting..."

"You were shouting."

"Aw, come on, Coach..."

"Let me ask you something. You know you're one of the top contenders for the Senior Award, right?"

"That's what they say." I felt myself deflating.

"I'm on the committee. Do you think I should support someone who can't keep his cool, who loses his temper in public, to be the outstanding senior of his class, to be named 'the kind of person the university aims to produce in scholarship, character, and leadership'?"

We stared at each other for a long minute, I hung my head, and mumbled, "Thanks, Coach," then turned and walked out, shaking my head, disgusted with myself.

Looking back, I wish I could have had sense enough to admit I was wrong. Over the years I've noticed that if you're quick to admit your mistakes, people usually are forgiving. Better to castigate yourself when you're obviously wrong than to defend the indefensible.

I worked hard to rebuild my relationship with my coach and teammates, but I had damaged my reputation with people I cared about because of my behavior. It was a lesson I'll never forget: If you can't control your emotions in an unpleasant situation, you don't deserve to have the respect of your associates. (I think Rocky must have been one of my supporters on the committee for the Senior Award, for I doubt I could have received it without his blessing. But he never gave me the satisfaction of admitting it even though we remained friends long after I graduated.)

Just as in the Nixon-Kennedy debate on TV, emotions often play a much more important role than logic or reason in persuading someone to see your point of view.

When I was twenty-eight, I left the computer industry for a year to become the field sales manager for Photostat Corporation in Rochester, New York. Though it was a big step up, giving me responsibility for twenty-seven branch offices in the United States and Canada, I wasn't thrilled about leaving Pennsylvania or the computer industry, and the constant travel was grueling, especially with two little children at home. I was willing to put up with it for the management experience, but one afternoon in a staff meeting I changed my mind.

The vice president said we needed to improve our gross margins on some products, and then, pointing his finger at each person in the room, asked, "What's the difference between a gross margin and a mark-up?" None of our product managers knew the answer. I was the last one he asked, and, fortunately, I knew. The vice president then began to excoriate everyone in the room but me, saying they were "gross incompetents," along with several other sneering epithets. They obviously were deeply embarrassed, and even though he complimented me, I was embarrassed for them. In fact, I was more than embarrassed. On the spot, I told myself, "I don't want to work for this man." Suddenly, returning to the computer industry and Pennsylvania became even more appealing. I quietly put out a few feelers, and within a month had an offer to rejoin UNIVAC as a manager in Detroit and another to become RCA's district manager in Pittsburgh. I might have spent my entire career in business in Rochester had it not been for my strong reaction to that moment when my boss treated our management team with contempt. A few years later, he became president of Photostat and flew to Pittsburgh to offer me the job of vice president. I said thanks, but no thanks.

He never knew why he failed to persuade me. Often we don't realize when we turn people off by our actions. When I left Photostat the only reason I gave was my desire to return to Pennsylvania. One of my mentors at UNIVAC previously had given me good advice when I discussed leaving that company: "Always go out smiling, for you never know when your paths may cross again."

Looking back on that episode, had my boss praised me for knowing the right answer rather than belittling everyone else in the room, they would have got the message without embarrassing all of us. It is never okay to criticize someone in public. Obviously, sometimes you have to disagree with someone privately, but the right way to do it is courteously, not dogmatically, and using the "sandwich" technique: Finding something sincerely positive to say, gently stating your disagreement, and concluding with another sincere, positive comment.

That approach worked for me in one of my first meetings with Speaker Newt Gingrich after Republicans won control of the House. My committee had jurisdiction over the Kennedy Center, on which I was a trustee. The Speaker informed me that we should slash their budget. "Taxpayers shouldn't be subsidizing tickets for rich people who attend the shows," he said. I met privately with him, told him I agreed that we shouldn't be providing such subsidies, and the good news was, we weren't. Public funding was limited to maintaining and improving the facility as a national monument to a president that, in fact, was the second most visited monument in Washington.

To Newt's credit, once he understood the facts he backed off and became a supporter of the Kennedy Center. Every time I visit or pass by the Kennedy Center, I feel a sense of satisfaction knowing that I played a role in preserving and improving it. If I had tried to push through its budget without making my case quietly and privately meeting with the Speaker, I probably would have failed.

> Dale Carnegie, the master persuader, wrote that there are six rules to making people like you: (1) Become genuinely interested in them; (2) Smile; (3) Remember a person's name is the sweetest sound in the English language; (4) Be a good listener. Encourage others to talk about themselves. You can learn something; (5) Talk in terms of the other person's interest; and (6) Sincerely make the other person feel important.

People want to be part of a team. There's a reason the preamble to the U.S. Constitution starts: "We the people..." *"We,"* not simply "The people." I dedicated my novel *Chances* "To my teams, in public and private life," because whatever success I've had both in business and in Congress has been due in large measure to the men and women who worked with me, supported me, and dedicated themselves to our common goals. They weren't employees or assets to be pushed around, but rather respected friends energized to achieve worthwhile objectives. In fact, building an esprit de corps; creating a positive environment, praising publicly or correcting privately; is important in every relationship.

I learned this through sports growing up, but the lessons carried over into college, management, Congress, and political campaigns. I was proud of my son, Bill, when he became the manager of a Goodyear store after college. At closing time, he would bring in pizzas so the employees—his team—could relax for a few minutes and talk about the day. The members of my various computer teams worked hard, but we hung out together, too. In Congress, we had our "Shuster Booster Softball Team" and the exhilarating challenges of many political campaigns and legislative battles bringing us together. Today, many members of our old teams are spread throughout the country, working for different federal agencies or private firms. We still keep in touch, and people often tease us about the "Shuster mafia." Now that I have retired from Congress, I've been touched by the warmth of continued friendships of my former colleagues and others with whom I worked over the years.

Yet I know I could have done a better job through the years if I had learned to control my impatience. When the good Lord passed out patience, he passed me by. I've always rationalized my low quotient by claiming, "If I had more patience, I'd still be working in the steel mill," but, of course, that's nothing more than a weak rationalization. Sometimes, one fault can lead to others. Due to my lack of patience, I'm often guilty of not paying enough attention to what others are saying, of not "schmoozing" with people. I'm too quick to correct. Although my family and friends might find it hard to believe, I have tried to improve, but it's a struggle.

You accomplish nothing by being abrupt. Listening and responding unhurriedly is worth the effort. I find it especially rewarding to encourage my grandchildren in their different endeavors, making a little game of whispering a "secret" in their ears, "Grandy loves you," even to the babies, Daniel and Jack. When, at three years old, Andrew and Jonathan fearlessly joined in with their older cousins to swing on a hanging vine off a hillside high above the ground on our annual boundary walk around the farm, I gave them both a special hug. Praise works wonders. Some compliments can last a lifetime.

My lifelong friend Mark Nagy and I were the storekeepers at the Iron City Fishing Club for the Objibwe Indian tribe in the Canadian North Woods one summer during college. At the end of the season we were invited to join the tribe for their final church service before they returned to the Christian Island Indian reservation. At the conclusion of the service, Walter Marks, one of the elders, rose and addressed us softly: "We must say goodbye, for we probably will never see each other again. But if we live good lives, we will meet some day in heaven." On behalf of the tribe, he presented Mark and me with delicately crafted birch-bark boxes the size of a deep pie pan, the lids stitched with bright red flowers and green leaves from painted porcupine needles. Walter continued, "In all the years we have been coming here to work, you are the only storekeepers who didn't cheat us."

A half-century later, I still have that box on my dresser in which I keep the small stones I gathered on my congressional travels around the world. And I'll carry the old Indian's compliment with me until the day I die.

A kind act can go a long way toward opening another's heart. Helmut Kohl, the strong-willed German leader who unified East and West Germany, told me that when he was a sixteen-year-old boy at the end of World War II, his family, along with most others, was in desperate straits, and the first suit he ever owned came out of an American CARE package. He would never forget what America did for him and for millions of other Germans after the war. Throughout his distinguished career he was unabashedly pro-American.

Often, kindness can overcome even strong differences. If people like us, it's easier for them to agree with us.

But whatever your message, it's got to be believable. One of our recent campaign slogans was "Bud Shuster is building for your

The summer I spent in Canada working with the Indians was one of the most enriching experiences of my life. I wrote a poem about it that I sent home, and recently came across it among my mother's keepsakes in her handwriting.

Discovering those long forgotten words brought back memories of the many kindnesses by those Indians toward two college boys far away from home:

CANADIAN SUNSET

Have you ever seen a sunset
upon the Canadian sky?
Viewed from the lake
the rapture brings a sigh.
The redness arrows downward
'till it meets the bluish cast,
a sight you'll forever grasp.
Your eyes mayhap grow dimmer,
Your hair shall fade snow-white,
But the thought of the Canadian sunset
Will kindle in you a light.
It seems one comes closer
To the Lord God from above,
You can feel his breath upon you
And sense his caring love.
The beauty of the lake
comes surely from somewhere.
Because it does exist,
implies God's loving care.
When the summertime is over
And back to the cities we go,
I'll think of the Canadian sunset,
And my faith in God will grow.

future." It communicated a positive message for your future, a constructive message about something of value to most people. And it was believable because of the evidence throughout the congressional district of the many major projects we had delivered through the years. Yet, had that been the slogan in our first campaign, it would have turned people off because I hadn't had the opportunity to deliver anything. Later, though, it was an emotional and factual positive reminder of our performance.

The slogan of our first campaign, displayed on billboards throughout the 9th District and in all our advertising, was "Bud Shuster believes in people." It was a warm, positive, introductory message; the first impression people got of this new guy who came out of nowhere. But they had to see me, to get the "feel of this fella" to believe in me. That's why our personal, door-to-door campaign was so important. We knocked on over 20,000 doors. Thirty years later, I still have people tell me, "I met you at my home during your first campaign." In any persuasive endeavor, there's no substitute for personal contact.

Whomever you meet and wherever you go in life, practicing the art of persuasion will carry you closer to your goals.

Chapter Four
Learning

Whosoever neglects learning in his youth,
loses the past and is dead for the future.

—Euripides

In the first semester of my freshman year at Pitt, I almost dropped out and enlisted in the Army.

I will be indebted forever to Mrs. Belfiglio, my freshman English teacher, for keeping me in school. One of our texts was a book of themes, and our mid-term assignment was to pick out a theme and write a paper modeled after it. A few days after we turned in our work, she called me into her office.

"Your theme was nothing more than a rewrite of one in the book."

"Well...ah...yes...like you said. I rewrote the theme using my words."

"I told you to write your own theme, using one in the book as an example."

She handed me my paper with a big red F scrawled across it. Stunned, I reacted, "I guess I misunderstood. I thought I was following your instructions."

"Well, you weren't the only one who didn't pay attention to my instructions. You and a half-dozen of your classmates all deserved an F."

I knew she had a reputation for being a tough grader, but she was going to sink me. If I didn't keep up my grade point average, I'd lose my scholarship.

"Can't I write another theme over the weekend and have you consider it?" I pleaded.

"What's done is done," she said. "I'll have to think about it. If you want to turn in another paper, go ahead. We'll see."

I was shaken. If I lost my scholarship, the prediction Dr. Hickes, my high-school principal, made would be right. I would be an embarrassment to everyone who knew me—and to myself. I couldn't let that happen. My life would be scuttled before it got started. Before I got kicked out of school, I would quit. I'd enlist in the Army.

My future was in Mrs. Belfiglio's hands.

That weekend, I immersed myself in writing and polishing a theme I called "Uncle Bill," about my uncle Bill Zeigler, a real character, who rose from farm boy to carpenter to the founder of Zeigler Lumber Company in Duquesne, Pennsylvania. After he retired, one of the rental buildings he owned needed a top floor window replaced, so, tying one end of a rope around the chimney and the other around his waist, he lowered himself down the outside of the building to make the repair. My aunt Elma, his wife, happened to be walking back from the store and spotted him. As he dangled in the air, she screamed, "Get down from there, you old fool, you'll kill yourself!" He nonchalantly waved to her, finished the job, lowered himself in through the window, and went home unfazed to a severe tongue-lashing.

Another time, he and Aunt Elma went with my grandparents on a picnic beside a shallow stream. Engaging in some good-natured horseplay, Uncle Bill ended up standing in the middle of the stream, splashing and laughing uproariously. Suddenly he dashed out of the water, threw himself on the ground, and yanked off his shoe. From underneath the innersole he extracted several sopping-wet hundred-dollar bills. While they ate their picnic lunch, he spread out the bills on the grass to dry.

And once when he was packing to go on a trip, he decided his long underwear would be too warm, so he took a pair of scissors and cut off the legs. Upon arriving at his destination and unpacking, he discovered he had cut off one leg and one arm. Undeterred, he proceeded to wear the underwear for several days.

After Mrs. Belfiglio read my theme, she handed it back to me without a grade, but with a note on it: "You certainly made this one original!"

I still didn't know what she was going to do about my grade, but I kept showing up for class, and working hard. To my surprise and relief, I ended up with a B in her class. I decided a good scare is often the best teacher.

I later learned that she was a friend of my high-school English teacher, Miss Birch, who taught night classes at Pitt. I think she may have interceded on my behalf. Miss Birch had introduced me to Edgar Allan Poe's *Gold Bug,* and even though I wasn't much of a reader in high school, I was captivated by it. My grandparents had a complete set of Poe's works that I devoured. That made me one of Miss Birch's favorites.

The extraordinary chain that led from Miss Birch to Edgar Allan Poe to Uncle Bill to Mrs. Belfiglio kept me in school. Luck was on my side.

The opportunity to complete my college education was, without a doubt, the single most significant determinant of how I would spend my life. Had I left Pitt, I probably would have ended up in a steel mill. Education opens up a world of opportunities. Without one, your choices can be extremely limited.

Getting a college education became my overriding goal. Growing up during the Great Depression in the Steel Valley of Western Pennsylvania, I saw the hardships suffered by people who were out of work. They often didn't know where the money was going to come from to pay their grocery bills, buy coal to heat their house, make their mortgage payments, or get a coat to block the winter chill. I remember a young mother sobbing in the alley a few doors from our home because the white baby shoes she had bought for her son had somehow fallen out of her shopping bag on her way home. A friend and I retraced her steps and found them. They were

Poll-Parrott shoes with the then-hefty price tag of $3.25. She started crying again when we knocked on her door, shoes in hand. She dug into her purse and offered us a quarter, but we refused, feeling noble.

Hard times make you appreciate the value of money, and so the value of a job. But it was clear to me even as young boy that most of the men who worked in the mills hated it. It was like entering a damn inferno every day. While they made relatively good money, there was no security. People got laid off all the time, and then the cycle of having no money started all over again. I realized that finding a steady job with good wages in a decent environment required education. That meant getting good grades to get into college, working at part-time jobs to save money, and if I was lucky, winning a scholarship. Getting an education was my ticket to the future. And surely, in this high-tech, fast-moving world, getting an education is even more important to achieving success.

After my grandfather died when I was eleven, a funny little gnome of a man named Mr. Caruthers came calling on my grandmother on Sunday afternoons. They had known each other growing up in Coal Valley on the Monongahela River, south of Pittsburgh. Though he had become quite wealthy in the coal business, his gifts and courtesies made no impression on Nana. But he made a great impression on me.

One Sunday afternoon, as I sat cross-legged on the living room carpet near him, he handed me a silver dollar and shook his finger, instructing me, "Learn something so you can earn something so you can have something."

He insisted I write the verse on a card and memorize it, promising another silver dollar if I could recite it when he returned. I did. It wasn't hard. And after reciting it to him the following week, I received my second silver dollar. I forget what I did with them. I probably wasted them on some foolish purchase, but I never forgot what he had me memorize. He was a wise old man, for you must learn something if you want to achieve anything. (Although money certainly isn't everything.)

Deciding what you want to learn is crucial. Like the lines in Robert Frost's famous poem *The Road Not Taken*: "Two roads diverged in a wood, and I—I took the one less traveled by, and that has made all the difference," figuratively, you choose a road when you leave high school. In some ways that choice sets a course for life. If you decide to go to college, your high-school record helps determine which schools will accept you. Should you go to a large university, a small college, or a trade school? What courses should you study? What are your interests and abilities? Those decisions will help determine your career path, many of your friends, and perhaps, even your partner for a lifetime, a co-parent for your children.

You can see that these early decisions can have enormous consequences and yet they often are made without much serious thought. Sometimes, they're based on someone else's casual suggestion or even on random chance.

It's scary for me to recall that at Pitt's freshman registration, I signed up for Army ROTC rather than Air Force ROTC because the line was shorter! I didn't think it made much difference. But that thoughtless decision changed my life. While I'm happy that it eventually gave me the opportunity to become a counterintelligence agent, which later helped qualify me for an appointment to the Congressional Select Committee on Intelligence, I certainly deserve no credit for a sound decision. It was dumb luck. I should have sought advice from upperclassmen or my father, who attended Staunton Military Academy in Virginia and served in the National Guard.

Deciding what field to major in also can profoundly affect your future. I wanted to go to law school one day, so I planned to take several courses in political science and history. But I discovered in a required freshman course that I had an aptitude for statistics, so I broadened my focus. More important, I went out for the Pitt debate team, and while it didn't appear on my transcript, debate became far more influential than my real major.

Although the illness of my parents and my need to earn a living kept me from law school, the debate team opened avenues for student leadership at Pitt and helped prepare me for the legislative battles I later faced in Congress.

There is no doubt that my opportunity to join the fledgling computer industry rested solely on my college record. It's enormously important to recognize that opportunities are based on the sequential building blocks we create for ourselves. Here's how my building blocks stacked up: My high-school record got me to Pitt. My Pitt record got me to the computer industry. A series of promotions in the computer industry got me to Washington and, ultimately, gave me the financial wherewithal to run for Congress. The point is that at each stage of your life, there is an opportunity to learn as much as you can. And each experience set atop another leads to opportunities and accomplishments sometimes beyond your fondest hopes.

The improbable story of how I joined UNIVAC also demonstrates how serendipity can affect your life. As my military service was ending in 1956, I was offered an attractive job with a company that marketed manual business systems. I was just about to accept it but thought it prudent to test the market to see if other opportunities existed in the same field. I sent my resume to the systems division of Sperry Rand, which somehow got misdirected and ended up on the desk of Mr. Hazzard, the regional manager of the newly formed UNIVAC division of the company. He called me in for an interview, but I quickly realized it was a mistake. I thanked him for seeing me but said I didn't know anything about computers and asked him to put me in contact with the manager of the systems division (which in those days produced and marketed a manual CARDEX system for keeping business records). Mr. Hazzard laughed and said, "Young man, almost nobody knows anything about computers. We'll send you to school...you'll be on the ground floor in a new division...in a new industry."

Even though I didn't know what I was getting into, the idea excited me, and I accepted his job offer. For the next year, they sent me to a series of programming schools, interspersed with on-the-job training at companies where computers were being installed. UNIVAC had given me an extraordinary education in an exploding new field while paying me a salary. I had to work hard to learn as much as I could but I never would have had the opportunity without my previous building blocks—and the lucky mistake of landing in Mr. Hazzard's office.

In the years that followed, whatever I achieved was based largely on what I learned during that first critical year, as well as on the guidance and knowledge of the many brilliant men and women with whom I was privileged to work in those early days of the computer industry.

Woodrow Wilson once advised: "Use not only all the brains you have but also all the brains you can borrow." I wasn't reluctant to "borrow" those brains around me, seeking advice from my colleagues, whose energy, commitment, and capabilities contributed mightily to our mutual success.

Some of the brightest people I have known, however, seemed to develop a very serious defect as a result of their intelligence. It might be called the "arrogance of intellect." A congressional colleague once said of a particular senator whom we both knew well: "Before I go into a room to negotiate with him, I remind myself that he's twice as smart as I am and as mean as a junkyard dog." We all were wary of him. Congressman John Anderson, who later left the Republican Party to run an unsuccessful third-party campaign for president, was defeated for a House leadership position because he exuded intellectual superiority. Congressman Richard Bolling, the brilliant Democratic strategist, never achieved his dream of becoming Speaker because he was widely perceived as being cold, arrogant, and not one to suffer fools.

There's a time to be smart, and a time not to appear too smart. One of Ronald Reagan's favorite sayings was, "It's amazing how much you can accomplish if you don't care who gets the credit." *Hubris* is a word that all too often describes people who think they are so smart they can get away with anything. Don't fall into that trap! No matter how much you learn, it's wise to recognize how much you don't know. There's an old Pennsylvania Dutch saying, "Ve grow too soon alt, und too late schmart." If you can acknowledge to yourself that there are important things you don't know, you can fill those gaps and display a little humility when you're with people who don't have all the answers.

Eventually, I realized that if I wanted to make my way up the ladder, I needed a better foundation in the principles of management. I read Peter Drucker's classic book *The Practice of Management*, in which he emphasizes that management is a professional skill, just like the practice of medicine or law. To be effective, one needs to learn various facets—accounting, finance, economics, marketing, human resources—and then practice them. He sold me. I enrolled in night school at Duquesne University to get my MBA. My graduate thesis was on marketing management.

Several years later, after RCA had transferred me to Washington, I decided to take a few doctoral level courses in microeconomics (the economics of the firm) and managerial analysis at American University. I got hooked, and ended up completing the doctoral program and writing my doctoral dissertation on "Selective Demand Determinants in the Computer Acquisition Process." On my doctoral comprehensives I received five out of a possible six "distinctions." (Sorry about the bragging, but I confess to a sin of great pride over getting my PhD at night while managing a major RCA operation.)

Without the knowledge I gained earning my MBA and PhD, without my continued learning, I would have been totally ill prepared to later become the president of Datel and then a founder of a software company.

Learning comes not only through education and reading but also through a broad range of experiences—and not just for managers. The educator John Dewey observed, "Education is not preparation for life. Education is life." What we learn in our youth can have value in later life in ways we cannot even imagine.

I've been blessed to be able to immerse myself in many different worlds: I grew up in the Steel Valley, came from a loving family, lived in both rural and urban environments, participated in sports, finished college and graduate schools, and was present nearly at the creation of the computer industry. Farming, raising horses, and hunting have kept me close to the earth. Serving in Congress, working with six presidents and their administrations, and traveling throughout America and the world, have been extraordinary privileges. Writing, speaking, teaching, consulting, working in businesses, and serving on corporate boards and as a trustee at two universities and the Kennedy Center in Washington, D.C., have taught me about the diverse culture and productivity of our country. I learned something from them all and relished the experiences. They enriched my life.

One of my most cherished memories is of working for two summers with "gandy dancers"—railroad track gang laborers. As Labor Day rolled around and the four college boys in the gang prepared to leave, a delegation of the regulars called me aside during our lunch break one day and said, "Lefty, the rest of those college boys can go back to school, but you belong out here with us." That compliment ranks right up there with all of my supposedly more prestigious awards. As one of the track gang, I got to know rough-cut rowdies, uneducated immigrants who were determined to send their children

I wrote a rather puerile little poem about our foreman when I was a gandy dancer, which I don't think would have made it into any book of poetry:

TRACK BOSS

Guisseppe Barardi is the foreman of our gang
The boys would like this track boss best
If from a tree he'd hang.
He says, "I geev you break today,"
But we all know a break from him
Will never come our way.
We say, "Perhaps he will be fair,
If we all do our part,"
But fairness in Guisseppe's mind
Is a foolish, stupid art.
The other day when Fats got hurt,
It didn't faze our boss.
He said, "So what, you think I care?
His pain no be my loss."
And so it goes from day to day,
From summer through 'till spring.
The boss to us is not a man—
He is an evil thing.

to college, convicted felons, drunkards, a black preacher, and a future Russian priest. I learned something from all of them.

Soak up as many different experiences as you can in life, and learn from them all. Equally important, learn by carefully observing the experiences of others, both good and bad. It's often been said that if we don't study the past we are doomed to repeat it. Likewise with the mistakes of others. Watch the people you admire. See how they live their lives. Don't hesitate to copy them. And also study those whom you don't respect. What have they done wrong? Resolve not to repeat their failures.

Miss Birch, my high-school English teacher, autographed my senior yearbook, "Don't forget what you already know." As we go through life we learn myriad facts and experience or observe hundreds of different situations, making it hard to remember all of the knowledge we have accumulated.

I regret that I did not keep my high-school and college notes, especially in history, French, and German. Once you have outlined a particular subject, referring back to those notes, even years later, can refresh your memory more easily than turning to a new and unfamiliar book. Had I been able to review my college German workbook before my trips to Germany, I'm sure I would have been able to communicate more effectively.

I also regret how I cheated myself in one of the advanced German courses I took at Pitt. Professor Schuck-Kolbein was demanding, requiring copious written and verbal translations. Professor Gnatkowski was a delightful man who required nothing more than reading aloud from German texts. If you showed up occasionally at the North Side German Club to have a beer with him, you were assured an A in his class. I chose the easy path with Professor Gnatkowski. If I had taken Schuck-Kolbein's class, I would have become more proficient in the language, and my later trips to Germany would have been more fun.

By the time I reached graduate school, I had learned the importance of saving my notes. I developed a system of jotting down ideas, quotes, or facts on 3x5 cards and categorizing them alphabetically by subject—from "America" to "Values." I still have my card files that

I used to study for my doctoral comprehensives. Preparing and keeping 3x5 cards has become a lifelong habit. I recommend it highly. I have used the cards to prepare my business presentations and congressional hearings and speeches. When I approached members of Congress on the floor to ask for their help on projects or issues before their committees, I would give them a card covering the subject as a reminder. One of my former colleagues recently teased me, "I thought we got rid of your 3x5 cards when you left, but your son, Bill, handed me one the other day."

I've also built a reference library over the years that includes encyclopedias, world almanacs, biographies, histories, a collection of "Great Books," and books on various subjects in which I am interested. (Recently, I've discovered that "googling" on the Internet is sheer magic.) I keep handy copies of Will Durant's *Lessons of History*, Ben Franklin's *Autobiography*, the Bible, and several other books for perusing. Lifetime reading can be a source of pleasure and inspiration. In addition to current events, I try to read some fiction or nonfiction every day, usually before bedtime. Try it. It will make your life richer.

Besides not keeping my notes, another regret is that at fourteen, I stopped practicing the piano, even though my cousin Sylvia continued to give me free lessons. On my Saturday morning bus ride to her home, I would scan my music lesson for the week, and then stumble through it, to her disappointment. I was totally irresponsible and ungrateful.

I now enjoy playing the piano and have found that listening to good music can work wonders. When I'm writing or working in my office, I enjoy background music, usually by one of the Russian composers—Tchaikovsky, Rachmaninov, Prokofiev—as well as Strauss waltzes and Big Band oldies. This might be a tough sell for me to the younger generation, but give it a try. Feel the energy and passion in Tchaikovsky's piano or violin concertos.

There is some evidence that certain music can help heal the body, strengthen the mind, and unlock the creative spirit. Don Campbell, in his book *The Mozart Effect*, offers dramatic accounts of how health care professionals and others are using music to treat anxiety, high blood pressure and pain, and to stimulate learning and memory. Students who sing or play an instrument score 51 points higher on SAT tests than the national average. (In fairness, that might be because smarter kids play instruments.) But there is no explaining away the physiological findings at a Baltimore hospital's coronary care unit: Half an hour of classical music produces the same effect as ten milligrams of Valium. Cows serenaded with Mozart give more milk. Classical music during English classes for immigrants speeds up their learning. Mozart's music may "warm up" the brain, according to Gordon Shaw, a theoretical physicist who conducts research on the relationship of music to intelligence. One study showed that lullabies calmed unborn children, while rock music "drove most fetuses to distraction...they kicked violently." There is mounting evidence that "babies—before and after they are born—are as responsive to music as the most avid concertgoers." Conclusion: Good music can enhance learning.

We also learned from my first campaign that snappy marching music can invigorate people and create enthusiasm. Another thing we learned: our music gave *us* more energy. We played patriotic tunes on a loudspeaker from our old campaign school bus as we traveled from town to town. We knocked on five hundred doors each day, sometimes staying in the streets long after the streetlights turned on until we achieved our quota.

I'm a proponent of the "use it or lose it" approach. There is evidence that even thinking can change the structure of the brain. Studies at the National Institute of Neurological Disorders demonstrated that the part of the brain's cortex devoted to the reading finger of blind people who use Braille is much larger than the same area in both blind and sighted people who don't place similar demands on their fingers. Dr. Edward Taub, a scientist at the University of Alabama, discovered that the cortex area devoted to finger movements increased significantly for musicians who play string instruments. The increase was greatest in musicians who began before the age of twelve, but, he reported, "Even if you take up the violin at forty, you still get brain reorganization." Playing the piano has been shown to delay the progression of Alzheimer's in some patients. The extraordinary point is that the brain rewires itself based on what we think and do. Deciding what we put into our heads, deciding what we choose to learn, is as important as what we choose to put into our bodies!

All these studies suggest that our brain is working subconsciously, not only during our waking hours but also as we sleep. I have often wrestled with a particular problem at work and then, as I left the office, dismissed it from my mind (or so I thought). The next morning, after waking up or during my run or sauna, a solution seemed to come to me effortlessly, without conscious thought. So sleeping on something is not just putting it off but letting your subconscious mind do the work for you.

We can exercise our brain just as we do our body. One of my close friends and debate partners at Pitt was Lloyd Fuge, who was blinded by a chemistry explosion as a teenager. We all marveled at Lloyd's prodigious memory. After something was read to him, he

My college friend Lloyd Fuge introduced me to the study of mnemonics, a technique for improving memory, recommending a book by David Roth, *Roth Memory Course*, which I have practiced since college. Roth wrote, "Visualizing, creating mind pictures in a systematic way, strengthens the memory."

Strong visual images are created by the following three principles: (1) Exaggeration; (2) Motion; and (3) Unusual mental pictures.

For example, if you meet a person and want to remember his name, repeat it immediately upon hearing it and associate it with another person you know who has the same name. Visualize the two of them shaking hands, or better, punching each other (exaggeration, motion, unusual). Or you might associate a name with a related visualization. See a Mr. Archer shooting an arrow, or a Mr. Shoemaker wearing a huge pair of bright, floppy clown shoes.

Association and visualization techniques can also be used in other ways. I remembered a 33rd Street by seeing Tony Dorsett, Pitt's all American, leaning against a street sign. His number was 33. Pictures are easier to remember than numbers. Poems can be memorized by visualizing key words connected to each other. Taking the time to study the Roth course or another like it will give you lifelong memory tools.

could recite back large passages. When fifty-two cards from a shuffled deck were called out to him, he could repeat them in order. Lloyd remembered hundreds of names and phone numbers.

As a young man, I made it a summer project to study and practice the Roth course. Eventually, like Lloyd, I could recite a deck of cards in the order it was flashed in front of me. I long ago lost that trick because I got lazy. I didn't keep practicing. But I practice the principles of association and visualization almost every day.

Learning to speed-read also can help us learn. When I was in my twenties, I bought a manual clicker device that flashed sentences at differing speeds before my eyes. It took about a month, practicing a little every day, to get my eyes adjusted to reading the fast-moving sentences. Even though I discarded the device years ago, I found that the technique was like learning to ride a bike or swim—once you get the hang of it, it stays with you. You can quickly skim a page and then slow down to absorb the more interesting sections. I'm sure there are much better speed-reading courses available today. I suggest you try one.

While techniques to help us learn can be valuable tools, only we can decide what is worth learning, what needs to be remembered. Learning is not only knowing facts and experiencing life but also deciding the relevance, the meaning, the importance of those facts and experiences.

The English poet Herbert Spencer wrote, "The great aim of education is not knowledge, but action." Like many great truths, that is an oversimplification. There are many different reasons for getting an education, for acquiring knowledge, for learning as much as we can. Knowledge helps us get a job, earn an income, and provide a standard of living for ourselves and our families. Knowledge helps us understand people and the world in which we live. Knowledge helps us make wise decisions about how we live. Knowledge gives us pleasure and enjoyment. Knowledge is power.

Learn as much as you can, for it will enrich your life in countless ways, far beyond what you might imagine as you begin your journey.

Chapter Five

Competing

The first biological lesson of history is that life is competition...we cooperate in our group— our family, community, club, church, party, "race" or nation—in order to strengthen our group in the competition with other groups.

—Will and Auriel Durant, *Lessons of History*

The drive to compete is part of human nature, and we must be prepared to compete in order to succeed—and, sometimes, even to survive.

When I was going off to Pitt, my high-school principal, Dr. Hickes, admonished me: "Understand, a university is a sophisticated jungle. It's survival of the fittest." I wouldn't put it in such stark terms, but college—and most worthwhile endeavors—contain a fundamental element of competition.

Competition is at the heart of our free enterprise system in America. Millions of individual efforts have produced material abundance unparalleled in history. Harvard economist Joseph Schumpeter said that out of the ferment of competition, new ideas and increased productivity and prosperity are created that later are replaced by even better ideas, higher productivity, and greater prosperity. He labeled it "creative destruction."

We Americans are so used to having the necessities, even the luxuries, of life, that it's easy to forget that in much of the world, people must compete to stay alive. We have become used to images of starving Africans scrambling to get their share of grain as it is doled out by UN humanitarian missions, or tribes attacking each other to gain control of land or natural resources. War, of course, is the ultimate form of competition and is a basic, agonizing part of human history. As a nation, we must be strong to compete in a dangerous world.

Even as children we compete for affection and sometimes for resources within our family. Although brothers and sisters usually defend each other fiercely against outsiders, sibling rivalry is a well-documented phenomenon.

As individuals, too, we must be prepared to compete. We compete in sports; we compete in business; we compete in government. Undoubtedly, life is more than competition, but it is successful competition that enables us to achieve many of our most important goals. Competition can be constructive or destructive, fulfilling or debilitating. We can refuse to compete or join in the game. Deciding when and how to compete are important decisions that affect both the quality and direction of our lives.

A childhood friend from a talented family had an older brother who was intellectually and athletically gifted. Everyone expected my friend to be like his brother from the time he was born. But his response was to not compete. Rather than study and play sports, he drifted through life. Ironically, he was bright and athletic. But somewhere, probably in his subconscious, he must have decided that he could not measure up to his older brother, that if he tried he would fail, and that the solution, therefore, was to not try. He ended up working in a local steel mill, loafing in bars, and setting a poor example for his children, who also are now drifting while their cousins are building productive and prosperous lives.

Much of my life has been spent in competitive environments, and I have felt the exhilaration of winning and the agony of losing. Interestingly, that supposed "agony" always became insignificant

> If you're willing to try and fail and try again, you cannot only achieve much in life but also experience the sheer joy of the effort, as Teddy Roosevelt stated superbly:
>
> It is not the critic who counts, not the man who points out how the strong man stumbled, or where the doer of deeds could have done better. The credit belongs to the man who is actually in the arena; whose face is marred by the dust and sweat and blood; who strives valiantly; who errs and comes short again and again; who knows the great enthusiasms, the great devotions and spends himself in a worthy cause; who at the best knows in the end the triumph of high achievement, and who, at worst, if he fails, at least fails while daring greatly; so that his place shall never be with those cold and timid souls who know neither victory nor defeat.

when compared with the elation of achieving a worthy goal. Even defeats have a way of opening other doors.

In the steel valley where I grew up, sports were a glorious part of life. There wasn't much else to do, and it was a good way to stay out of trouble. It diverted people's minds away from the realities of unrelenting poverty and a world at war. For the best athletes, it was a ticket out of the valley's mills and mines. For others, who trudged out of the steel infernos each day and headed to the sandlots, sports actually gave their lives meaning.

I'm sure I owe my love of athletic competition and physical fitness to my two older cousins—Lloyd and Hartley Greinert. They were among my earliest childhood heroes. Both labored in the mills, but Lloyd later became a policeman and my Sunday-school teacher. He was really tough, but the worst word he ever used was "cripes." After making a drug bust one Saturday night, he awoke the next morning to find the body of his informant dumped on his porch. That was as close as anyone ever came to tangling with him. Lloyd played semi-pro football and described trying to tackle the great football star and Olympic athlete Jim Thorpe as "like getting smacked by a falling block of granite." He attended all my basketball games, even when on duty. (He said the high-school gym could be a dangerous place and needed police protection.)

I sat for hours on the couch with Lloyd, thumbing through his scrapbooks, marveling at the exploits that were pictured. Years later, toward the twilight of his life, my children watched, wide-eyed, as he got on the floor and did several one-arm pushups.

Lloyd had a ferocious competitive drive that made him push himself to excel. It's a quality inherent in most great athletes—and in most successful people. Ted Williams, probably the greatest hitter in baseball, whose .406 batting record hasn't been matched in over seventy years, *had* to win. He paid enormous attention to detail, studying the pitchers he was going to face, scraping grooves in the bat handle to improve his grip, and sanding the stem to increase the whip effect. Competition is more than being emotionally energized to win. It includes being mentally alert—being willing to study the competition.

Competition is also more than beating someone. Sports teach sportsmanship. There's an old sports aphorism: "It's not whether you win or lose, but how you play the game." But that isn't totally true. Football coach Vince Lombardi said: "Show me a good loser and I'll show you a loser." Winning is very important! But how we win also matters. Nobody likes a cheater. When Sammy Sosa got caught "corking" his bat, even though he claimed it was only for batting practice, it stained his otherwise stellar record. The discovery that respected historian Doris Kerns Goodwin had allegedly plagiarized some of her writing undermined a lifetime of work. The scandals surrounding some corporate executives and union bosses have tarnished the images of both big business and labor.

Being a team player is also essential. I place great emphasis on creating a team atmosphere, an esprit de corps. Yet, I made a big mistake in forgetting that principle when I was negotiating the sale of Datel and my interest in C-3, our software company. Though we worked hard to build two interlocking management teams, when the opportunity to sell Datel arose, I was so hellbent on making the deal that I didn't include our C-3 team in the discussions. To make matters worse, University Computing Company, with whom I was negotiating, insisted that I sell my stock in C-3 as part of the deal to make them a substantial minority stockholder. I was so focused on doing the UCC deal because they had the capital we needed, I forgot the advice that Datel's major investor, Randy Smith, had given me as a rookie CEO: "When negotiating, the bottom line is always leverage."

UCC had the leverage on me, and I caved to make the deal. And in so doing, I let down one of my teams. When I told them, after the deal was done, they were hurt and angry. A few weeks later, they decided to increase the stock ownership of an outside investor who was on the board. I thought it was a bad decision. I believed that investor would try to gobble up the company.

I expressed my strong misgivings about their decision, and finally told the C-3 management team that I wanted them never to forget that at exactly two o'clock on that particular Friday afternoon, I was advising them not to go through with their plan. I felt certain they would lose control of the company we had created (in my living room), and they eventually would be pushed out. It was a tense meeting, and they were not about to accept my advice. We had been a team, and I had failed them. They were right. But because they were angry, they made a bad decision.

Within two years, C-3 was sold to a larger company and they were out. While they made some money on the sale, the dream— our dream—of building a mega-software company never came to be. I will always deeply regret that I did not include them in our negotiations. Because of that failure, my second failure was my inability to persuade them that they were about to make a serious mistake.

If you're on any kind of a team in life, especially if you're the captain, don't let down your teammates.

When a high-school teachers' strike threatened the football season for my son, Bob, and his teammates, he appeared before the school board on behalf of the team to urge them to allow non-teacher, substitute coaches so they could continue the season. He risked the anger of the teachers because he put his team first. (Later, the principal told me: "That team would follow Bob off a cliff!")

Teamwork calls for leadership, but sometimes the most important competition is challenging yourself, whether it be in sports, business, or highly personal objectives. I like to check my cholesterol once a month with the goal of keeping it under 200. It's a motivating tool. I'm competing against my desire to eat the wrong foods. Try setting your own personal challenges. It works.

Another thing I've learned is that if you want to succeed, you have to be willing to take risks. I would not have become a vice president of RCA's computer division had I not been willing to turn down the job without the title. Nor would I have been elected to Congress had I not been willing to compete against an entrenched opponent. I would not have been elected to the Republican leadership as chairman of the Policy Committee had I not been willing to challenge Congressman Bill Frenzel, a more senior member who already was in the leadership as chairman of the Research Committee.

Counting primaries, general elections, GOP conventions, and internal congressional elections, I've won fifty-three elections. However, with risk comes inevitable defeat. I lost an important election to my good friend Senator Trent Lott when we ran against each other in 1980 for whip, the no. 2 position in the Republican leadership. It was an intense campaign that I lost by three votes—fair and square.

But it was a chance to learn. My post-election analysis showed that I had done several things right: I had been a strong voice for our party positions through my chairmanship of the Policy Committee; I had met privately with every member to ask for his or her vote; I had visited many districts to support important transportation projects; and I had helped several members raise campaign funds.

I also had made several political mistakes: As chairman of the Policy Committee, I had exercised my prerogative to sit on the Personnel Committee rather than let Congressman Ken Robinson remain in that position. That cost me his vote. I had supported a resolution denying Congressman Richard Kelly of Florida Republican campaign contributions because of his involvement in the ABSCAM scandal, where six Democrats and one Republican eventually were convicted of accepting bribes from an FBI undercover agent posing as a rich Arab sheik. That cost me some Florida votes. And I had supported Gerald Ford in the Republican presidential primary over Ronald Reagan. This cost me some conservative votes. In retrospect, I was lucky to come as close as I did, but it hurt a lot at

Bud Shuster, chairman of the Republican Policy Committee, witnesses President Jimmy Carter's signing of the historic embargo against Iran during the hostage crisis

the time. (Trent and I have remained close friends over the years, and he was very appreciative of my support when he lost his leadership position in the Senate over his remarks about Strom Thurmond's segregationist past. It was a bum rap. But in politics, as in life, there are a lot of bum raps. Expect them.)

Following the whip election, I sat down and put my thoughts on paper.

I Like Myself Better

When I lost the whip race by three votes, I learned something about myself. I had been worried about how I would handle a loss. I was fearful that I would not react with grace.

I was surprised at how calmly I reacted. When the vote was announced, I immediately went to the podium, gave a little speech that was totally supportive of Trent, and moved that a unanimous ballot be cast for him. I received a standing ovation and several commented that I had displayed "great class." I surprised myself.

A few supporters and my senior staff took me out for lunch where they drowned their sorrows, but I stuck to Diet Coke, wanting to be sure I controlled my emotions. I then pampered myself by buying a pair of very expensive running shoes, ran a fast mile in the gym, and took a call from President-elect Reagan, who wished me well and commented on how many elections he had lost.

We never should be completely satisfied with our performance. By trying to do better, we become better. Painful as it is to lose, I have always tried to learn from my mistakes, whether it was for whip or eighth-grade class president—my very first race. When my good friend, Oliver Dudley, and I competed for the presidency, he received 14 votes and I got 12. I voted for him because I thought it was the sportsmanlike thing to do. After the election, he told me he had voted for himself. Had I also done so, the election would have been a tie. We would have flipped a coin, and I could have won. Years later, we had a good laugh about it, but it also taught me a lesson: Don't give away anything to your opponent.

In politics, as in life, people are motivated to make decisions by a variety of factors. Self-interest is number one, but jealousy, friendship, common values, past slights, loyalty, and intuition can all lead people to act as they do.

And yet in most competitive situations, it is wise to keep your emotions in check. I've seen people let their emotions override good judgment. As a result of reapportionment in 2000, Congressman Frank Mascara's district was redrawn. The Pennsylvania Democrat could have run in a newly created heavily Democratic district or in a reapportioned district that today includes most of Democratic Congressman Jack Murtha's old district. Frank blamed Jack for carving up his old turf, even though it wasn't true—Republicans drew the map—and in anger, Frank chose to run against Jack rather than in the new district where he had a shot at winning. Though Frank's friends tried to dissuade him, his pique got the best of him and he was badly defeated.

It's so easy to get caught up in strong emotions; it's important to listen carefully to the dispassionate advice of trusted friends. And negative decisions based on revenge are the worst kind.

Especially in public life, there is a tiny fraction of people whom I would define as "haters." They *need* to be negative, to lash out, to stridently oppose. As Harry Truman said, "Any jackass can kick down a barn, but it takes a good man to build one." I have witnessed elected officials who are perpetually on the attack. They have a mean streak in their character.

In my first campaign, the opposition paid a small weekly newspaper to print a "smear" paper against me, and hand-delivered it to 80,000 homes. On the cover was a picture of me inside a phony three-dollar bill. They claimed that our cattle were diseased, our horses were starving, the farm clothes I was wearing in a picture actually were tailored designer jeans, I had been a poor student, and that my wife was a member of the wealthy Pugh family (life would have been easier if that were true!). When my supporters confronted one of the Democratic county chairmen involved in the attack, his response was, "I am not above gutter politics."

As a rookie who had never run for public office, I was shaken. But the good news was that the preposterous allegations caught the attention of the responsible media and greatly helped my campaign. The owner of the largest radio station in Altoona challenged the publisher of the unscrupulous paper to debate me on air.

The debate attracted a huge audience. While the publisher railed at me, I methodically laid out the evidence to refute his wild accusations: the health certificates for our cattle; my high-school and college transcripts; my family background and Pennsylvania roots.

Eventually, the moderator stopped us, announcing that the station had investigated the accusations and found them to be totally false. It blew the lid off the campaign. Over the next several days, newspapers across the district came out in support of our campaign. I should have paid the opposition to attack me. Out of that experience came three lessons: first, it's better to confront your attacker than ignore him; second, be sure of your facts if you attack an opponent; and third, if you want to compete in that kind of arena, brace yourself and your family, because, as the legendary comic strip character Mr. Dooly said, "Politics ain't beanbag."

I've also tried to follow the admonition "When attacked, calmness, not temper is the key." But that's easier said than done. Politics is a blood sport.

Speaker Tip O'Neill told the story of how, as a young state legislator, he went against his leadership on an important vote, even though he was a good "party man." Although they were not pleased, they learned that they couldn't take him for granted. He had achieved a degree of independence.

I was in a similar situation my freshman year. We were faced with a historic vote on the War Powers Resolution requiring the president to seek congressional approval before committing U.S. troops to combat. President Nixon vetoed the resolution, and congressional Republicans were expected to support his veto. Many freshmen had been elected on his coattails and so discussed the issue at length in our freshman class meetings. After wrestling with the decision for several days, I took the position that we should override the president's veto because the Constitution gives war-making powers to Congress.

On the day of the vote, Gerald Ford, our Republican leader, sat down with me in the chamber and asked me to sustain the veto, emphasizing the importance of the vote. I told him that while I understood, it was only after much reflection that I felt I had to vote to override it. It was a matter of *conscience*. Jerry shook his head, patted me on the knee, and said, "If it's a matter of conscience, you vote your conscience." (That was a measure of the man who became the 38th President of the United States.) When I spoke during the debate to urge a vote to override, I said, "I consider this the single most important vote I have faced in this chamber...it is the people who bleed and die, and what affects the lives of the people should be decided by the representatives of the people."

We overrode the veto by four votes, with 23 of our Republican freshmen joining me. Of the more than 12,000 votes I recorded, I still consider it to be one of, if not the, most important vote I ever cast. It also sent the message that, even though I was a conservative Republican, I would be my own man. Once I made my decision, nothing could have changed my mind. Years later, when I fought the transportation trust fund battles, several of my colleagues expected me to buckle under the pressure, but the thought never occurred to me.

In fact, unlocking the transportation trust funds was the longest and most competitive, not to mention most significant and gratifying, battle of my congressional career. It began when I was a freshman, and culminated in victory twenty-five years later over the opposition of both my own Republican leadership and the Democratic President of the United States.

It was lucky for me that when we began the floor debate on the Highway/Transit bill in 1973, Don Clausen, the ranking member of the subcommittee and a manager of the bill on our side, was called to the White House for a meeting. He looked around, saw me sitting behind him itching to speak, and thrust his notebook at me, saying, "Here, you handle this."

Bud with President Gerald Ford at the signing of one of his transportation bills

I was thrilled at the opportunity and even happier when we defeated a major amendment to divert more funds out of the Highway Trust Fund and passed the bill.

Soon after that, Congressman Clausen rose on the floor of the House and put a statement in the *Congressional Record* praising my "persuasive performance on the Federal Aid Highway Act of 1973," noting that my participation in the debate "was a key factor in maintaining the integrity of the Highway Trust Fund."

Thus began my mission to stop the diversion of money away from the transportation trust funds for unrelated purposes. We ultimately unlocked the highway, transit, and aviation trust funds so they could be spent on improving transportation. The stakes were high: thousands of lives would be saved, millions of travel hours would be eliminated, and hundreds of thousands of jobs would be created.

I'm convinced that the opportunity to participate as a freshman in that major debate led to others. First, I was tapped to become a member of the Chowder and Marching Club, a prestigious group of Republican members, founded after the Second World War by several junior Republican congressmen, including Gerald Ford, Richard Nixon, Mel Laird, and John Lodge. Three or four Republican freshmen are invited to join in each new Congress. Our class included Trent Lott of Mississippi, who eventually became majority leader of the Senate, and Jim Martin of North Carolina, who later became governor. Membership in C&M is for life, and the club includes two presidents, a vice president, a House Speaker, senators, governors, and cabinet officers. I was the fiftieth member elected in the club's history and the first and only Pennsylvanian, until my son, Bill, was elected. Some of my closest friendships grew out of my C&M experience.

I was also made the ranking member of the Surface Transportation Subcommittee in my second term. Traditionally, the ranking member of the full committee held that position because it is the largest subcommittee. At our organization meeting, ranking member William Harsha of Ohio surprised everyone by announcing that he was stepping down from the subcommittee position. If none of the senior members objected, he said, he would like to appoint me. No one had time to object—the deal was already done. Afterward, everyone wanted to know how I had pulled it off. But I was as surprised as they were.

As the ranking member of the subcommittee, I honed my knowledge of transportation issues through the years, eventually becoming the ranking member of the full committee.

On the morning after the 1994 Congressional elections, as I was recovering from minor surgery in Walter Reed Hospital, I received a telephone call from my friend Norm Mineta, a Democrat from California and chairman of the committee, who greeted me: "Good morning, Mr. Chairman!"

The new Republican control of Congress positioned me to set the transportation agenda. My goal of unlocking the transportation trust funds could become a national priority. But how could it be achieved with the Republican leadership, other powerful committee chairmen, and President Clinton opposing it?

It was a question I couldn't afford to dwell on. I couldn't pass up the opportunity to wage this important fight. I was the chairman. And it was my responsibility to the people of Pennsylvania and the country to make the goal a reality.

As House Republicans organized the Congress for the first time in over forty years, most chairmen wanted to reduce the size of their committees to make them more manageable. I took the opposite tack. Ours became the largest congressional committee in history, with seventy-five members. I knew that if Minnesota Democrat Jim Oberstar, my ranking member, and I worked together to keep the committee bipartisan, we'd start the battle with seventy-five votes when we went to the floor with legislation.

On January 7, 1995, at the beginning of the new Congress, Jim and I introduced "The Truth in Budgeting Act," which would require that the four user-financed trust funds be spent for highway/transit, aviation, inland waterways, and harbor maintenance purposes, rather than diverted to unrelated programs. We emphasized that the nation's transportation infrastructure needs were staggering: highway and transit systems were inadequate; the air traffic control system was still running on vacuum tubes; the inland waterways system, with its outdated locks, was clogging river traffic; and our ocean ports needed to be deepened to handle modern vessels. Perhaps most important, countless lives could be saved by building safer highways and modernizing the air traffic control system. And for every billion dollars spent on the highways, approximately 70,000 jobs were created.

The war began.

We lost the first battle. The day before the Budget Resolution was to be brought to the floor, I announced that I would be offering an amendment, supported by my entire committee, to increase highway spending out of the trust fund by $12 billion. I had been assured by the House leadership that I would be given a fair shot, though I later learned that what they meant was that I would be given a fair shot as long as they thought I would lose. That afternoon when it became clear that I had a 30- to 40-vote lead, all hell broke loose. At the White House, even President Clinton got on the phone to pressure Democrats to vote against us. The Republican House leadership called an emergency conference that evening to urge defeat of my amendment. Chairmen of the powerful Budget, Appropriations, and Ways & Means Committees attacked the amendment, strongly suggesting retaliation against any member who supported me. As I defended my position in front of the conference, I felt like Daniel in the lion's den.

When the vote came the next day, we lost by two votes. Yet, had we won, that probably would have been the end of our goal to permanently unlock the trust funds. Because we would have received a $12 billion increase for that fiscal year, members would have been unwilling to go through a future battle for another change in the law. By coming so close to victory despite all of the arm-twisting opposition, we proved that we had broad-based, bipartisan support. I was not going away. We had just begun to fight!

Jim Oberstar and I led a bipartisan group of members with superb staff support headed by Jack Schenendorf, my committee chief of staff. We built a coalition including governors, mayors, state legislators, county commissioners, the highway and transit lobbies, labor unions, environmental and safety groups, the Chamber of Commerce, the Black Caucus, and the Conservative Action Team. I had to make several compromises to hold together such a broad coalition, but with the president and the leadership against me, it was the only way we could muster the votes to achieve our fundamental objective. There would be no compromise on unlocking the trust fund.

I crisscrossed the country, meeting with state and local leaders to learn their priorities and to announce their support for our legislation. In Oklahoma City, for example, I met with Governor Frank Keating to inspect the intersection of I-40 and I-35, where a state trooper had fallen into a gigantic hole in the bridge. These interstate highways had been built to carry 60,000 vehicles daily, but were actually carrying twice that number, more than half of which had out-of-state licenses. The problem clearly was more than a state problem; it was a national one.

Back in Washington, I met individually with members to commit my support for their high-priority projects, and our staff worked to be sure their requests met our qualification criteria.

It took a year of intense effort, but by the time we went to the floor with our legislation in April 1998, we had overwhelming support. When the vote came, we won by a veto-proof 343 to 80. Even the leaders and several of the chairmen who originally had opposed us, were finally with us.

The Senate followed with strong bipartisan support led by Senators John Warner, John Chafee, Robert Byrd, and Max Baucus. I chaired the House-Senate Conference that reported out our final negotiated version. It passed the Senate 88 to 5, and the House 297 to 86.

President Clinton changed his position and announced his support. As I stood at his shoulder when he was signing the historic legislation into law, he looked up at me smiling, and I smiled back, thinking: now you're acting as if this was *your* idea! But that was just fine.

The long and sometimes lonely battle had been won. The major trust fund had been unlocked and $218 billion, the largest transportation bill in history, would improve the nation's highway and transit systems, correcting problems that were costing the country thousands of lives.

At one point when both the president and the leadership were still against us, Congressman Nick Joe Rahall of West Virginia came over to me in the chamber and said, "Bud, we want you to know how much we appreciate your efforts, but we understand, with all the pressure, if you'll have to cave in. We won't think anything less of you."

I shrugged and replied, smiling, "Nicky Joe, I may get beaten into the ground, but the thought of caving in never entered my mind!"

Looking back, I'm convinced we won because we had strong arguments on our side, we were willing to compromise on several policy issues, and we had organized a year-long, unremitting, national campaign to build support. We never could have achieved our TEA-21 victory had we not shown genuine respect and attention to the opinions and needs of our colleagues. We dedicated ourselves and our energies on achieving a worthy goal. It's a formula for accomplishing good things in life.

I've seen powerful members of Congress get badly defeated on big issues because they overplayed their hand and were unwilling to negotiate or to build broad coalitions. Occasionally, an exaggerated sense of self-importance—of hubris—led them to think they could roll right over people. It's a recipe for defeat.

Many said that unlocking the Aviation Trust Fund would be even harder because aviation did not have the same broad national support enjoyed by highways and transit. Actually, it turned out to be easier. We had set the precedent and established the principle that trust fund user taxes should be dedicated to their intended purposes. AIR-21, which unlocked the Aviation Trust Fund to provide $40 billion to improve America's aviation system, passed the House and Senate overwhelmingly, and was signed into law by the president on April 5, 2000. But not without a few tense leadership sessions.

In one meeting on March 23, 1999, Majority Leader Dick Armey commented that they couldn't permit my language unlocking the Aviation Trust Fund to be offered on the floor because "If we do, he'll win."

To which my good friend Majority Whip Tom Delay responded, "And if we don't, he'll bring down the pending budget resolution."

Proof once again that leverage works. If they thought I was bluffing, they would have rolled right over me. Build a reputation for standing your ground, and people will take you seriously.

I've had my share of battle scars along the way, but I wear most of them proudly. In becoming chairman, I was subjected to two painful experiences that I could not let interfere with my opportunities to pass historic legislation. Although I clearly understood that as one rises to a position of authority, he becomes a target for the opposition, I nevertheless was surprised by the attacks when they came.

Several years earlier when we were in the minority, then Chairman Jim Howard of New Jersey and Speaker O'Neill asked me to give my bipartisan support to a major transportation project in Boston known as the "Big Dig." I studied it and came to the conclusion that it was, indeed, crucial for the future not only of Boston but the entire Northeast. Although it was controversial, I backed the project and got to know many of Boston's leaders, who became my supporters. As the years went by, although the future benefits of the project remained solid, the cost escalated dramatically. Accusations were made concerning the propriety and legality of the construction and land acquisition contracts, and eventually the U.S. Attorney's Office in Boston launched an investigation. Although my involvement in the project was scrutinized as part of an extensive investigation, the U.S. Attorney ultimately issued a letter stating that I was neither a target nor even a subject of the investigation.

That didn't stop the media from pouncing on the story. There were those who dearly wanted to hang my scalp on their belt. Good people were hurt by an overzealous investigation, and although I was pleased to get a clean bill, the experience was unnecessarily distressing.

Even more painful was the brush with a group sponsored by my old nemesis, Ralph Nader. The Nader group got three liberal Democrats to endorse their letter of complaint against me to the House Committee on Official Standards. It triggered a four-year ordeal that cost a tremendous amount of time and money.

Finally, in October 2000, I took the floor to announce that I would accept a "Letter of Reproval" from the committee acknowledging four minor points, including, for example, that a junior staffer had taken time off to work in our campaign without documenting that she had made up the time.

I quoted Jim Hansen, chairman of the Standards Committee, who had come to me exactly two years earlier to inform me that after conferring with the other members of the committee they agreed there was nothing of substance in the Nader group's charges, that they were "B.S." (He didn't use the initials.)

Under the rules, the "Letter of Reproval" was the mildest form of criticism. Webster's dictionary defines "reproval" as "to scold or correct usually gently or with kindly intent." That certainly was not the way I felt! It galled me to accept even the four picayune claims, but it made sense to bring the costly ordeal to a close.

The Nader people angrily said, "It's not even a slap on the wrist." To me, however, I likened my feelings to Thomas Jefferson's response to accusations against him while serving as governor of colonial Virginia: "It is a wound in my spirit which will only be cured by the all-healing grave."

In retrospect, I made several mistakes. Several of my colleagues had urged me to immediately take the floor and counterattack when the Nader group made their complaint. I should have fought back. When we finally did, we got the committee's attention and settled the matter.

Fighting back also *feels* good!

The price of public life requires a thick skin, and Harry Truman's admonition applies: "If you can't stand the heat, stay out of the kitchen."

Throughout my many battles in Congress, I've tried to follow the advice of British Prime Minister Margaret Thatcher, which I highly recommend: "Stay focused on the positive things you're trying to accomplish."

After winning our trust fund battles, the last major piece of legislation I was able to shepherd into law was the largest environmental restoration project in history—the restoration of the Florida Ever-glades. While the driving force behind the project was Congress-man Clay Shaw and other Florida members, I was pleased to move the legislation through my committee and the House. I held it up temporarily until we got agreement to include funding to help over two hundred small communities across America improve their water and sewer systems. Leverage works!

I wish we could have fought the battles to unlock the Inland Waterways and Harbor Trust Funds, but 9/11 put those issues, along with many others, on the back burner until more settled times.

Serving as chairman of the Transportation & Infrastructure Committee and as the ranking member of the Select Intelligence Committee gave me the privilege of competing in the world's most important arena—the people's House of the greatest nation on earth.

It gave me the opportunity to improve and strengthen America, while working with many wonderful men and women for whom I have the greatest respect—men and women who make great sacrifices to serve their country.

Francis Bacon wrote: "The power to do good is the true and lawful end of aspiring." Competition is the spark that fuels our aspi-rations. Choosing where, when, and how to compete is a lifetime challenge. But compete we must, for if we don't, the world will pass us by.

Picture of Bud Shuster's portrait hung in the Rayburn
building of the Capitol upon his becoming chairman of the
Transportation & Infrastructure Committee

Bud meets with President Leonid Kutchma of the Ukraine during a congressional trip

Chapter Six
Energizing

The world belongs to the energetic.
—Ralph Waldo Emerson

Our energy level helps determine how much we are able to accomplish in any given day—and throughout our life. We might intend to play ball with our kids, go for a run, complete a project at work, or finish a book, but we won't get there if we don't have the energy. Our physical fitness, mental attitude, and general health combine to pump us up or slow us down.

As my mother lay in a hospital bed with both legs amputated above the knee as a result of a blood clot, she emphasized, "Always take care of your health. If you lose your health, you've lost everything." Back then, we didn't know much about the danger of high cholesterol and being overweight or the benefits of exercise. But the heartbreaking experience of watching a dear, kind, gentle soul go through months of agony focuses one's attention on healthful living like nothing else can.

My mother's loving lecture struck me especially hard. I was twenty-five years old, and fat!

I ended basketball season my senior year in high school, weighing 154 pounds. At graduation, three months later, I weighed 160. By the time I finished college, I was up to 170. Three years later, after military service and several months of UNIVAC programming schools, I stepped on the scales outside my mother's hospital room and topped 201 pounds. How could I, active in sports most of my life, have let myself turn into a bowl of jelly? Embarrassed by my lack of discipline and motivated by my mother's suffering, I resolved right then, staring at the scales in the hospital, to fix the problem.

The next day I joined the Pittsburgh YMCA. Not knowing exactly what fitness regimen I wanted to follow or what was available at the "Y," I strolled through the facilities, eventually wandering behind the handball courts. I noticed an older gentleman smacking a ball against the walls by himself. Seeing me peer in the small window, he motioned me to come in and asked if I would like to play. I told him I had never played the game. Actually, I had never even seen anyone play handball.

"I'm Bill Gorman," he smiled, sticking out one of his gloved hands. "Come in. I'll teach you."

And he did. We became noontime handball buddies. He was a retired widower who spent his days playing handball and his evenings ice-skating. He was in such good shape, he could have been a senior tri-athlete. As I raced around flailing at the ball, he would glide from side to side in the center of the court, hitting bank shots off the four walls, floor, and ceiling.

I fell in love with the pace and aggressive style of the game, and after I got the hang of it, I became a pretty fair player. Over the next two decades, with handball as the core of my fitness regimen, I brought my weight back under 160. As I traveled around the country throughout my computer years, I regularly worked out and developed handball pals across America. It's sinfully prideful to report (but I can't resist) that neither of my two athletically talented sons ever beat me on the handball court, even though I offered to buy each a car if he did. (They eventually got their cars with my help, anyway.) Although handball gave me enormous pleasure, when I entered Congress, I quickly discovered the House gym—and the unfortunate fact that it had no handball courts. It became difficult to leave the Hill or to find partners who fit my early morning schedule, so I took up running and lifting weights instead. I have followed my

Bud plays handball at the "Y"

new fitness program for over a quarter of a century. I developed some of my closest friendships with fellow "gym rats." Liberal or conservative labels melt away when you're pumping iron beside someone or running with them on the National Mall.

My congressional trips took me to cities around the world, and running gave me an up-close look at different cultures—not to mention some surprising experiences. In Poland, as we began our run on the streets of Warsaw, the acrid smell and taste of coal dust, the eye-stinging soot permeating the air, the raw sewerage spewing into the Vistula River, carried me back to my boyhood in the Steel Valley. Maybe the environmentalists had a point, I thought. The doctor with our delegation handed us breathalyzers as we came back in wheezing. The next day, I wet a red bandana handkerchief and tied it over my face, startling several Poles as I ran by.

In Pakistan, as we prepared to run through the embassy compound, a Marine guard told us to stay in the center of the road to avoid the lethally poisonous snakes lurking in the nearby bushes. If we were bitten, he said, we had approximately two minutes to get back to the infirmary for the antidotal shots or we would be dead. I was happy to share the center of the road with the embassy vehicles.

In Moscow, with two feet of snow on the ground and a temperature of twenty-below-zero, I decided to run back and forth between opposite corners of my spacious but dilapidated room in the National Hotel on Red Square, facing the Kremlin. But as I pounded my way across the floor, the door burst open and in barged two soldiers, rifles lowered. They took one look at me, shrugged to each other, and backed out. I'm sure they thought, "Crazy Amerikanski!"

I always tried to top off my workout with a sauna. When I told a friend who is part Chickasaw Indian how relaxing I find a sauna at the end of a workout, he said that he, too, took a sauna nearly every day. Smiling, he looked me in the eye and exclaimed, "It's more than relaxing—it's a spiritual experience!"

I agree. There's something about the dry heat that clears the mind. Creative ideas and solutions seem to effortlessly tumble out.

Although I haven't seen any medical research to prove it, I'm convinced that sweating away impurities and re-hydrating oneself with several glasses of water daily, has got to be good for the body—and maybe the soul, too. In our sauna at the farm, every time I splash water on the rocks out of the wooden bucket that my son, Bill, and I got in Finland, it brings back fond memories of that frigid trip, which culminated in a celebration of Bill's twenty-first birthday in Moscow.

My fitness program energizes me, adding quality and, I hope, longevity to my life. I began reading books and articles about fitness, and I like to think I'm a student of the subject. I've learned that getting your pulse rate up for about thirty minutes several times a week and building muscle tone are both important. It's probably fortunate that I switched from handball to running at the age of forty because many of my friends who continued playing handball, squash, or tennis, eventually required hip or knee replacements. In fact, six years of basketball, twenty years of handball, and over thirty years of running finally have taken a toll on my legs. I now alternate between running and riding a stationary bike. We can't completely escape the wear and tear on our body, but we can use common sense to care for it. In high school, I took the padding out of my first-baseman's glove to get a better grip on the ball, and now, fifty years later, when I press against my right thumb or squeeze a tube of toothpaste, I feel an arthritic jolt. I'm paying the price for not being more prudent.

Making fitness my hobby has paid great dividends. When my neck was broken in a car accident in 1982 (I was wearing my seatbelt!), the neurosurgeon explained that I needed two major operations: one to put in Mylar pins and the other to transfer a piece of my hip bone. The seriousness and length of the operations meant I would require at least a two-week recovery period between operations. But just three days after the first operation, he came into my room at the Bethesda Naval Hospital and said, "Your body's recovered so quickly, we can do the second operation tomorrow if you're game."

"Let's go," I replied. I wanted to get out of there as fast as I could.

Within a week, although I was heavily dosed with pain killers, I was able to go home for Thanksgiving, loaded onto a mattress in the back of a station wagon.

At the end of that holiday weekend, two staffers loaded me back into the car and drove me to the Capitol, where I was taken in a wheelchair onto the House floor. As a manager of a major transportation bill, I stood up eighteen times to speak. But as the debate ended and I attempted to step out from behind the manager's table, my knees buckled. Fortunately, two of my staffers caught me and steadied me because I insisted on walking out of the chamber.

Just a week later, as I was being pushed in my wheelchair onto a plane headed for Jamaica to deliver the keynote address to the American Bus Association, I resolved to go cold turkey off the pain medication. I spent two days and nights shivering under the blankets in my bungalow before my speech, but on the appointed day, I instructed the staff, "Get rid of that wheelchair. I'm walking to the hall."

In the coming weeks, I began gently pedaling a stationary bike. It took me six months to gradually regain my strength and get back to running, but had I not been in shape prior to the accident, the operations and the recovery would have been much harder. It's even possible I may not have survived the surgery. And had I not been wearing my seatbelt, there is no doubt that I would have been killed. I count my blessings every day. A few months after I recovered, it was especially disappointing and ironic to learn that the internationally respected neurosurgeon who operated on me was in a car accident that left his hands paralyzed. When I visited him in the hospital, I couldn't resist asking if he had been wearing his seatbelt. He slowly shook his head and replied, "No." How tragic that one thoughtless act of omission had ruined his career.

People often comment about how disciplined I must be to religiously follow my workout regimen, but the truth is I deserve no special credit. It requires no discipline. I love it. It's my "drug" of choice. If I miss my morning workout, I feel lethargic all day. Many of my House gym buddies agree. Somehow, expending energy actually increases energy.

Increasing your energy level through exercising, however, is only part of any well-rounded fitness program. Dr. Kenneth Cooper, considered the father of aerobics, thought that no amount of exercise makes up for bad nutrition or obesity. "Your diet is the foundation upon which your total physical and emotional well-being is based," he wrote.

Exercising is easy for me, but following sound nutritional advice is not. I love to eat. I think "diet" is a dirty word. People go on diets, but eventually slip back into their old bad eating habits. It has taken me half a lifetime to figure out how to manage my eating habits. I try to follow what Cooper calls a lifetime "Positive Eating Plan" (PEP).

Fad diets come and go, but we can't ignore a fundamental physical law: There can be no weight gain when output of energy equals caloric intake. Counting calories matters. So does the quality of food we put into our bodies. Sometimes, I've paid more attention to the quality of oil I've put in my car than to the junk food I've put in my body.

Nathan Pritikin, a health guru who was far ahead of his time, wrote *The Pritikin Program for Diet & Exercise* in 1980. I still thumb through it regularly to remind myself of the benefits of good nutrition and exercise and the destructiveness of animal fats, sugar, excessive alcohol, and sedentary living. Certainly, red meat, whole milk, cheese, and butter can raise our cholesterol level. The famous Framingham Heart Study demonstrated that a person with a cholesterol reading of 240 is three times more likely to have a heart attack than one with a reading below 200. It also showed that too many sugary foods can lead to obesity, which, in turn, raises blood pressure. A person with a systolic blood pressure of 160 runs four times the risk of a heart attack compared with one below 120.

One of the ways I've motivated myself to eat properly is to set targets for my weight and cholesterol level. I get on the scales every morning, and in addition to my annual physical and fitness tests, perform home cholesterol and blood pressure tests monthly.

Another thing that motivates me: I've observed that when I overeat, although I get a momentary gratification, I not only gain weight

> Regularly recalling a few scintillating sayings helps keep me motivated to follow my diet and exercise regimen:
>
> Make less thy body and more thy grace. (Shakespeare)
> Obesity and stupidity are synonymous. (Chesterfield)
> I'm angry for what you are, a great, fat glutton. (Faust)
> A fat paunch never breeds fine thoughts. (St. Jerome)
> Obesity is highest among the lower class. (Harvard study)
> You can't eat what isn't in the house. (Shuster)
>
> Thomas Jefferson described his prescription for a long life in a letter to his nephew:
>
> "Give about two hours every day to exercise for health must not be sacrificed to knowledge which is a desirable possession, but health is more so. I eat little animal food: vegetables are my main diet: few glasses of weak wine, five to eight hours sleep and good moral reading one-half hour before sleep. Always rise with the sun."

but also feel sluggish and require an extra hour of sleep the next day. That means, in effect, I'm losing 6 percent of my waking day. If I stuffed myself two days a week, I'd be losing 104 hours a year—the equivalent of about one week. (Similar projections can be made about the impact of wasting time.)

Probably, nothing can be more injurious to our health than smoking or excessive drinking. Fortunately, I don't have to worry about smoking because my basketball coach cured me of that in high school. If you're thinking about lighting up, consider the consequences: The American Cancer Society reports that over 250,000 people die annually from smoking. Pritikin calls it "slow-motion suicide."

Excessive alcohol can also take a terrible toll. It destroys the liver, causes red blood cells to stick together, reducing the blood supply to the heart, kills brain cells, depresses the immune system, and impairs judgment. From my time as chairman of the Transportation & Infrastructure Committee, I know too well that the mistakes it can cause are not benign. About half the fatalities on our nation's highways are alcohol related. Over the years I occasionally drank too much, and I'm convinced I've done more dumb things in those situations than in any others. One of my friends stops drinking during February every year. He says he does it just to make sure that he can control his drinking. (But note that he chooses the shortest month of the year.)

Apparently, a little red wine each day can help our cardiovascular system, but the trick is not to use that as an excuse for over-indulging. I usually limit myself to one or two glasses of wine at dinner and make it a rule not to drink during the day. I follow an old Army saying: "Not until the sun has passed over the yard-arm."

Besides keeping bad habits in check, managing our stress level and mental attitude also plays a key role in maximizing our energy level. Stress can be positive. When our adrenaline starts pumping as we begin a speech, take a test, make a business call, or play a game, our stress level rises in a way that can actually sharpen our performance. It's when we become frightened or angry that our stress level spikes negatively. Keeping focused on positive goals can turn stress into an ally.

The evidence is overwhelming that positive thoughts produce positive results—and negative thoughts produce negative results. *The Journal of the American Medical Association* recently reported that "Women who believed that they were prone to heart disease were nearly four times as likely to die as women with similar risk factors who didn't hold such fatalistic views." It's called the "nocebo" effect: Think sick, be sick. Medical research is discovering that our attitude can actually strengthen or endanger our immune system.

Hugging also apparently works! Dr. Delores Kreiger, the author of *Therapeutic Touch*, established in her experiments that "when ill people are treated by the laying-on of hands, a significant change occurs in the hemoglobin component of their red blood cells." Another study shows that "the immune systems of both healer and healee are enhanced through the process of therapeutic touching."

So does laughter. Norman Cousins, professor of Medical Humanities at the UCLA School of Medicine, came to a related conclusion in his research: "Determination and purpose enhance the immune system...laughter is inner jogging." I try to practice what these wise people teach—to keep my head filled with positive thoughts—and I hope you will, too.

Both my parents died at the young age of sixty-four. Worse, they were both in ill health for about the last ten years of their lives. I'm convinced the reason I've outlived them and that I'm in good health is because I've taken advantage of the medical knowledge that has emerged in recent years. I wish I'd done a better job earlier in my life, and even now it is an ongoing challenge—albeit a happy, worthy challenge! As baseball great Mickey Mantle quipped, "If I'd known I was going to live this long, I would have taken better care of myself." Actually, I have no complaints, and think I've done a pretty decent job.

The benefits of a healthy lifestyle are incredible. I feel great. I'm able to be productive, to continue contributing to worthy endeavors—not the least of which is building for the future of our family. There are even financial rewards. After I passed a recent physical exam, the insurance company put me in the "preferred-plus" health category, which increased the value of my policy by 25 percent with no increase in the premium—passing along the eventual benefits to my children and grandchildren.

I know life can take strange twists, and I could be gone tomorrow. But I'm still here today and loving it! You, too, can reap the benefits of a healthy lifestyle. Take care of yourself, and the odds are that you will live a long, healthy, and happy life!

Don't waste time, for that is the stuff life is made of.
—Ben Franklin

When the great Babe Ruth hung up his spikes, he was sure he could fulfill his dream of becoming the manager of the New York Yankees. After all, he was the "Sultan of Swat," the greatest homerun hitter in history, and Yankee stadium justifiably was dubbed "the house that Ruth built."

As he confidently sat down with Colonel Jacob Ruppert, the Yankees' owner, Ruth assumed it was simply a matter of negotiating the terms of his contract. But Ruppert reportedly looked him in the eye and said, "Babe, what makes you think you can manage a major league baseball team? You can't even manage yourself."

Ruth had a reputation as a carouser, with uncontrollable appetites for food, booze, women, and boisterous fun. His roommate on the road was asked once what it was like to room with Babe Ruth, and he replied, "Well, to tell you the truth, I actually roomed with Babe's suitcase most of the time."

Babe's dream was denied because he couldn't govern himself. Despite his legendary athletic ability and extraordinary charisma, he failed to manage the days, hours, and minutes of his life. He who would control the world must first learn to control himself.

In our little church in Glassport, when I was growing up, there was a pleasant, distinguished gentleman who seemed a cut above everyone else. Yet he was looked upon askance—and even despised by some—because he was a dreaded "efficiency expert" in the steel mill. His job supposedly was to squeeze more work out of the men. Years later though, I realized that he wasn't pushing them to work harder, he was pushing them to work smarter. He was an industrial engineer who did time-and-motion studies to help workers become more productive. It reminded me of my first day on my ditch-digging job after high-school graduation. The foreman showed me how to use my legs as leverage under the shovel handle to make my work easier. It struck me then that if there is even a trick to digging ditches, there must be harder or easier ways of doing almost everything in life. We all should pay attention to our own efficiency as we manage our daily lives.

It has taken me a lifetime to turn the knowledge of men and women wiser than I into a coherent plan to manage myself. And I quickly confess to being only partially successful. Nevertheless, this short chapter may be the most important of the book, for, even though you may nod your head in agreement with what I've written—believing, achieving, persuading, learning, competing, energizing, managing, saving, protecting, and bonding—if you don't translate those ideas into daily action, I will have failed in my effort to help you make the most of your life. How well you spend your time will determine how much you can accomplish in your life. The word "daycare" usually applies to children. But how you take care of each day—your "day care"—provides the basis for achieving all your goals.

I suggest you read Ben Franklin's *Autobiography* as I did at Pitt. It gave me a framework for organizing my life. When I went to work at UNIVAC, I decided that the punch cards then in common use with computers could serve as "day cards" for me. I had a batch printed, which I have used to plan each day for nearly half a century. My system works for me, and I recommend you develop your own system to manage your time.

At the start of each year, I take a little notebook and write down my goals (some of which may change as the year progresses). For example, my family goals might include guiding and encouraging our grandchildren, improving Shuster Lodge, and working to provide a base of financial security after I am gone. My public goals include being a good citizen, contributing to worthy causes, performing "pro bono" work, and reaching out to my friends. My spiritual goals may be trying to be a better person through prayer and reflection. My intellectual goals usually include stimulating my brain through reading, writing, thinking, watching constructive TV, practicing the piano, and listening to classical music. My financial goals could include working on worthy projects that provide good value to my clients and my firm and living within a reasonable budget. My fitness goals always include exercising, eating properly, keeping my weight around 155, and my cholesterol level below 200.

I recently had a stunning revelation about my Positive Eating Plan, an idea I adopted from Dr. Kenneth Cooper's book, *The Aerobics Program for Total Well-Being.* I've prided myself on eating nutritious foods, low in cholesterol, animal fats, and triglycerides, and counting calories to keep my weight down. But, recently, my blood pressure, which always has been excellent—around 115/75—began creeping up. I told the doctor I was mystified because I was eating well and exercising regularly. He assured me that my annual physical tests were all good, but asked, "How much salt are you consuming?"

"Gee, I don't know, but I don't put any salt on my food," I boasted.

"Check out the sodium in the processed foods you're eating," he suggested. "Sodium causes high blood pressure, which damages the heart, brain, kidneys, and eyes."

When I read the labels on the foods I was ingesting, to my astonishment, the low-calorie, low-cholesterol, frozen dinners, salad dressings, sports drinks, pretzels, and even some of the bread and cereals, were loaded with sodium. For example, I had discovered a salad dressing that contained zero calories and cholesterol, so I was pouring it over my salad *and* my baked potato nearly every evening. Nothing wrong with that. Right? Wrong! The sodium content was astronomical. My supposedly "perfect" foods were almost perfect but for the potentially lethal ingredient they contained.

I immediately replaced processed foods with unprocessed ones, and began counting milligrams of sodium just as I count cholesterol and calories. Within three weeks, my blood pressure was back to normal.

What a dummkopf I had been! I, who prided myself on my supposedly good nutrition, who had spent almost a lifetime working at it, had been oblivious to an essential element. My inattention to detail almost had caused a serious health problem. It reminded me of something the owner of a successful Chrysler car dealership once told me: "There are twenty-eight lines on the dealer monthly financial report required by Chrysler—everything from gross sales and profit to expense details—and failure to pay attention to and control any *one* of those twenty-eight performance measurements can sink you."

So it is with life. We may think we are managing something well, but our inattention to even one detail can eventually scuttle us.

I try to focus on the details of managing my day by dividing the day into twelve steps. Each night, before I go to sleep, I fill out my day card for the next day. Over the years, while my responsibilities

---

This is one of the mantras I repeat during my sauna each morning:

Excessive alcohol is a drug and a poison that destroys my brain, destroys my liver, and turns me into less than I want to be. I will drink alcohol only for my health and well-being, which means I will drink only one or two glasses of wine at dinnertime.

I have no desire to put any refined sugar in my body, which stresses my pancreas, raises my triglycerides, contributes to serious disease, and makes me feel bloated and uneasy. I have no desire to eat ice cream, chocolate, cookies, candy, cakes, pies, or pudding.

I have no desire to put animal fats in my body—red meat, whole dairy products, fried and fatty foods, butter and oils, which raises the cholesterol in my body, clogging up my veins and arteries, causing serious disease and premature death. And I watch my salt intake. (Recently added.)

Instead, I'll have the strongest desire to achieve each of my 12 steps to purify my mind, my spirit, and my body on this wonderful day.

1. Rise at 6 AM, rested, feeling great. Weigh myself. Have my early morning routine of hot water, toast and coffee. Record my calories.

2. Exercise my body by running or biking, and open my mind to the wisdom of the world and my spirit to God. Give thanks for my many blessings (see morning prayer in Chapter One). Do my back exercises, crunches, pushups, weights and take a sauna. Cool off, shower, drink 16 ounces of water, and listen to my Board of Directors who advise me how to live my life:

   Jesus: Love the Lord thy God with all thy heart and all thy soul, and love thy neighbor as thyself. Earn thy neighbor's love and love thyself constructively.

   Franklin: Make your virtues daily habits.

   Jefferson: It's wonderful how much we can do if we are always doing.

   Lincoln: Embrace great principles and never let them go.

   Churchill: Never give up! Never ever give up! Never ever, ever give up! Fight on!

   Mama: Love the little ones as we have loved you.

   Family: Give your loved ones roots, and guide them on their way.

   Cooper: Your diet is the foundation upon which your life is built or destroyed.

   Drucker: Concentration is the key to economic results. Concentration is the key to results in life. Concentrate on worthy goals.

   (If I can follow their advice even some of the time, I'll be a better person for it.)

3. Work efficiently on my projects. 10 AM: toast, coffee and water. Record calories.

4. Continue working.

5. Noon: perfect lunch: Oatmeal, fruit, soy-milk, vitamins, water. (Restaurant: Diet Coke and large salad.) Record calories.

6. Continue working. 2 PM: coffee.

7. 3 PM: ten minute break, and review day plan.

8. 4 PM: banana and tea. Record calories.

9. 5 PM: swim, farm work, hike, practice piano.

10. 6 PM: perfect dinner: Sparkling water, salad, oil & vinegar, chicken or fish, vegetables, baked potato & lemon, fruit, glass of wine. Record calories.

11. Evening: relaxing with friends and/or family, reading, TV.

12. 9 PM: sparkling water & Granola bar. Bed: read, TV, review day and plan tomorrow. Record calories. Give thanks for the day. Asleep at 10:30 PM.

    (I put a check or star after each step as I achieve it.)

PROJECTS

1. Revise Ch. 10
2. Call A.A.R.
3. Plan B.E.P. Meeting
4. Invoices R'vd
5. Emily—Honor Roll
6. Invite Members—Dinner
7. Review FIN
8. Horses Hay
9. Call F/S
10. Call M/T

have changed, my routine has remained remarkably consistent. Your day plan will be different from mine, but the important thing is to have one. (An example of the front of my day card is on page 109 and the back is shown on the left.)

After my workout in the morning, I shave in the sauna, and visualize my day plan in detail. The sauna puts me in a relaxed, almost hypnotic state, as I silently remind myself of how I want to live to maximize my life, and to savor every minute of that God-given day.

If I succeed in following my day card, I will have achieved several important goals, which makes me feel good about that day. I probably achieve all twelve steps of my day plan 90 percent of the time. My behavior, perhaps, is best described by the saying about the little boy: "When he's good, he's very good, but when he's bad, he's awful." Writing down my day plan helps motivate me to keep me positively and productively structured. I highly recommend that you develop your own. It will improve your life. Guaranteed!

I also carry a card in my wallet with aphorisms on it that I refer to occasionally:

Carpe diem (seize the day!)
Believe and achieve.
The only thing I have complete control over is my attitude.
My ambition is to be of some use in this world. (Bertrand Russell)
Temperance in prosperity is a measure of virtue.
Seldom do you exceed your own expectations.
Nothing is too hard for thee. (Jeremiah)
Only today can be perfect or poor, for tomorrow never comes.

Several self-help experts recommend that we latch onto a mantra that we repeat to ourselves as a motivational tool. Perhaps the most famous is the one recommended by Emil Coue, the French psychologist: "Every day in every way I am getting better and better." One of my favorites is: "I'm eating only perfect foods at only the proper times, and savoring every minute of this God-given day."

When I discovered I needed to reduce my sodium intake, I focused on a temporary mantra for a few weeks: "I'm eating nearly no salt today to maximize my life."

Make up your own mantra, repeat it to yourself through the day, and change it periodically to keep it fresh. Say it to yourself when you wake up and before you fall asleep. Say it when things get tough, when you've done something wrong, when you've done something right, when you don't know what is right or wrong. Say it when you are about to lose your temper, curse the world around you, or after you stub your toe. Say it when you embark on a great adventure, face an awful choice, or confront an awesome challenge. Let your mantra seep deep into your soul, and it will give you strength to be a better person. Positive thinking works.

If you're like me, when you're walking somewhere, often your mind wanders or is simply blank. It's a good time to repeat your mantra, or focus on your day plan.

Besides having a mantra, it also helps to set short-term goals. Be prepared to re-set your goals and start over if you fail. For example, the Pritikin diet book has a thirteen-day plan. If I start it and slip, I start over.

One of my biggest challenges is to eat properly because I love to eat—especially sweets. I could eat a quart of ice cream and go back for more. But I don't anymore. I use my day card and a mantra to help achieve my eating plan. It has taken me years of trial and error to finally discover an eating plan that I enjoy, and I'm still finding ways to improve, as my recent discovery of the evils of sodium attests. Contrary to conventional wisdom, eating a big breakfast doesn't work for me. It just keeps me hungry all day. The PEP I've described in my twelve-step day plan fills me up, provides excellent nutrition, and tasty food. In fact, my noontime oatmeal, smothered in luscious fruit, is my favorite meal of the day. I have no trouble sticking to my PEP most of the time. Develop your own Positive Eating Plan. It will add happy, healthy years to your life.

When traveling, you can save a lot of time and keep on your Positive Eating Plan by being what I call "self-contained." I bring instant coffee, a heating element, sodium-free bread, Granola bars, instant oatmeal, powdered milk, and fruit with me. I eat breakfast, and, if possible, lunch in my room. I'm also hooked on keeping fifteen-calorie, sugarless, hard candy with me. It's my "cheating" food. I don't count the calories, and I pop a piece in my mouth any time I feel like violating my PEP.

Though my approach to managing my days may not work for you, I hope it will motivate you to think through how you might best manage your life. But manage it you must, or you will wander through life like a piece of driftwood, bobbing uncontrollably in swirling waters. By managing my day instead of letting the day manage me, I have time to achieve my goals, enjoy my family and friends, experience the joy of being alive, and touch the lives of others.

Life passes too quickly, at best. *Carpe Diem!* Seize each day!

Chapter Eight
Saving

Whatever you have, spend less.

—Samuel Johnson

Ten money jars bearing the names of our grandchildren line a shelf in my den. When the children turn three, they get their own jar, and they know they can fill it by helping me with chores around the farm. It's a joy to watch them loading firewood in the wagon, pouring grain down the chute to feed the horses, or washing the four-wheelers after their parents take them on a ride through the woods. When their work is completed, they race to the closet for their jars and report to me for their pay. We have an understanding that they should save at least half of what they earn. This is how I have tried to teach them the value of money. Children never learn the value of money if their parents—or grandparents—lavish them with unearned allowances. Similarly, we always required our children to perform household chores for pay and to find part-time jobs when they became teenagers. Require your children to earn their allowances. You will be teaching them an important value, for which, someday, they will thank you.

But they also need to know that money isn't everything. People sometimes misquote the Bible, saying, "Money is the root of all evil." But that's not what the Bible says. Paul, in his letter to Timothy, wrote: "The love of money is the root of all evil."

There is a vast difference between the two statements. If we are consumed by the thirst for money, if we structure each day around the pursuit of money, we lose sight of far more important values: our relationships, our opportunities to be a positive force in our communities and our country, and our ability to achieve a sense of purpose and fulfillment in our lives.

Stories abound about people who "have everything" but whose lives are in shambles. They are driven, anxious, unhappy souls. Their intense, uni-focal vision has turned their lives into one long quest to acquire more—more money, more material goods, more financial power—often at the expense of their families and their own emotional and physical health.

But as someone once observed, the only people who can say money doesn't matter are those who have it. Of course it does. People use money to achieve productive, balanced lives. Our standard of living for ourselves and our family depends on the ability to earn a decent income.

Deciding what standard of living you hope to achieve will help define your career goals. In this wonderful land of ours, getting an education makes it possible to achieve a comfortable, mid-range income. If you set your sights on reaching an upper-income bracket, business or one of the professions are your most likely routes. But don't count on becoming a multimillionaire. The probability of achieving that goal and the emotional price you may have to pay to get there make it a likely pipe dream. If it happens—congratulations.

But whatever you decide to do, be sure you have a passion for your choice. You'll only really succeed if you do what you love.

Confucius wrote: "If you would be happy for a week, eat a fatted pig; if you would be happy for a year, marry a pretty girl [or handsome boy]; if you would be happy for a lifetime, love your work." And, unless you are in dire straits, no amount of money is worth spending your life in a job you hate. Reject any vague, romanticized notion of a career you don't thoroughly understand, or a direction others may be pushing you against your judgment. We had several pharmacists in our family, so I was nudged in that direction, but the idea held no appeal for me. And when the good Lord passed out spatial perception, he passed me by, so I knew I would make a poor engineer. Thankfully, I followed my own instincts.

Personal satisfaction is not solely measured by money. In education, government, or non-profit work, you won't become wealthy, but you can find a deep sense of fulfillment, reasonable financial security, and free time for your family, friends, and outside interests. Our daughter Gia gave up tax accounting to become an elementary schoolteacher, which she loves. Although our family's net-worth declined substantially during my congressional career, no amount of money could have equaled the privilege of serving my country and the people of Central Pennsylvania all those years.

People make a terrible mistake when they see their work as drudgery. Sometimes it can't be avoided, but satisfaction can be found even in menial tasks. I loved being part of a railroad track-gang—working out-of-doors in the summer with the sweat pouring as I hammered spikes deep into the ties, keeping time to the tap-tap tintinnabulating rhythm with my partner on the other side of the rail. Admittedly, I would not have wanted to do it for a lifetime, but you can learn something from every job along the way. For me, working at different jobs as a young man, spending two years in the military, seventeen years in the computer industry, twenty-eight years in Congress, and farming, teaching, and writing, have added vibrancy to my life.

But whatever career you end up in and however much money you make, be sure your standard of living is based on your income, not what you wish it were. One of the most common mistakes people make is trying to live beyond their means.

It's easy to charge things, but if you can't pay your bills on time, you'll end up being saddled with double-digit interest rates. You will lose your credit rating, and the respect of your associates, if you don't pay your bills on time. Even worse, you may have bill collectors hounding you, trying to repossess your house or your car.

Once, as a teenager, when my father was out of work, I was at home alone when the mailman delivered a registered letter to my parents, which I accepted. I shouldn't have opened it, but I did. It was from a Pittsburgh department store informing them that their past-due bill was going to be turned over to the sheriff for collection. Naively, I telephoned the store and pleaded with them not to send the sheriff. I promised I would begin making monthly payments out of my $2.50 paycheck from Samuels shoe store and the $3.00 I earned weekly from mopping the floor at Miller's drug store after school. When I told my parents what I had done, they were embarrassed and assured me they would scrape together the money to pay the bill before the sheriff came knocking.

The story shows how much stress money problems—whether you're living from paycheck to paycheck or struggling to pay your bills when you're out of work—can put on a family. Some nights my father would stand looking out the window, unable to sleep, and our financial worries were a constant strain on my mother.

Like my family, most Americans suffered during the Depression. Growing up in that difficult time, I witnessed good families struggling to find work, put food on the table, clothes on their children, and stop foreclosures on their homes. It made an indelible impression on me. I resolved to become financially secure. I worry that a new and more affluent generation does not appreciate the importance of saving or grasp the gravity of being without necessities. I focused on carefully managing my money even as a teenager. I hitchhiked and brown-bagged it to McKeesport to work at Samuels shoe store during high school to save money to buy a car. When I went off to Pitt, although my academic scholarship paid my tuition, I continued to work at the shoe store on Saturday and got summer jobs to cover my other expenses. I also lived frugally. Beeman's chewing gum cost five cents, and by tearing a piece in half, I could make a pack last a week. I kept a detailed record of every expenditure (which I still have). My first semester, I spent $347.20. I still shine my own shoes. It takes less time than going to a shoeshine stand, and I probably save a few hundred dollars a year.

My second semester, I learned one of the most important financial lessons of my young life. When my Grandmother Shuster died, she left me a $1,000 insurance policy that would be paid to me when I turned twenty-one. The owner of our corner car repair garage had a spiffy 1946 Dodge club coupe that could be mine for $800. I sharpened my pencil and calculated that eighteen dollars a week should cover all my car expenses as well as the repayment of a bank loan, a sum I could earn by transporting six of us students between Glassport and Pittsburgh for $3 each, per week. With my heart in my throat, I asked for a meeting with the president of the local bank, located above where my grandfather's barbershop had been. I explained my plan and offered the insurance policy as collateral. He grilled me about the details of my calculations, and then said, "Well, if you're Elmer Greinert's grandson, I guess you're a good risk."

I had saved $270, so I borrowed $530 secured by the insurance policy to make my first big purchase. I easily found five riders, and every week we each put $3 in a can in the glove compartment of my car—*my* car! The investment worked out perfectly. I repaid the loan on time, and had a car for college. That first thousand dollars taught me the importance of having money to invest and of going into debt only if the purchase would generate enough cash to repay the loan. (The exception is the purchase of a home, which upgrades your life style and probably increases in value over time.)

In managing your personal finances, don't make the mistake of ignoring the fundamentals of planning, budgeting, and investing. Today, when middle-income people get into financial trouble, usually it's not because they have inadequate income but because they don't manage their money wisely. A good rule is to live *below* your income. Pay yourself first. Set aside 10 percent or more of your income every month.

Through the years, I treated our family finances like a business. I established a budget each year based on my expected income and expenses, counting saving as an "expense" that had to be paid just like the mortgage and the water bill. Each month I penciled my income and expenses on my "E. G. Shuster & Co." income statement and updated the balance sheet. It took only about thirty minutes, but the exercise forced me to focus on our family's financial status. More important, it put me in the habit of saving.

One of Aesop's fables tells the story of the ant and the grass-hopper. On a cold winter night an ant was dragging out some corn he had stored during the summer. A starving grasshopper saw him and begged for a little corn. "What were you doing all summer?" the ant asked.

"Oh, I had a grand time singing," the grasshopper replied.

"Well," said the ant, "since you could sing all summer, you may just dance all winter."

Bad times learn what good times saved. If bad times come, and one prudently should assume they might, for life can be full of unpleasant surprises, financial security can spell the difference be-tween survival and bankruptcy. Saving—accumulating fixed and liq-uid assets—should be one of your highest priorities.

I set a goal of having enough liquid assets to cover a year's expenses if I were ever out of a job. We lived frugally, and by the time I became an RCA vice president, I had achieved that goal. I probably would not have taken the risk to leave RCA and become president of a start-up computer-terminal company had I not pro-vided for our financial security in case that venture failed. With a growing family, doing otherwise would have been irresponsible. When I put together my management team, I emphasized that they should be financially prepared to be out of a job within a year. (The fear of failure can be a great motivator.) Nor could I have taken the huge risk of running for Congress without having a nest egg to fall back on. Some of my most important opportunities were predicated on having lived frugally and saved conscientiously.

What I didn't do was borrow money to run for Congress.

As Shakespeare wrote, "Neither a borrower nor a lender be, for loan oft loses both itself and friend...." The irony in loaning money to people is that they become embarrassed if they cannot repay it and often resent being in your debt. I made it a rule not to loan money to anyone except family members. (To qualify for a Shuster loan you have to meet two conditions: it has to be for a worthy cause, such as buying a home or investing in a sound business; and you have to have a plan to repay the loan.) Over the years it has been a special joy to be able eventually to turn those loans into gifts to our children.

There's a farmer's saying, "Don't eat your seed-corn," meaning, when a farmer's corn crop comes in, the first thing he should do is set aside enough for planting the next year's crop. Likewise, it's vital that you not dip into your investments if you want to achieve financial security. Spend part of the income from them, if you must, but "never eat your seed-corn" except in dire emergencies.

My Grandfather Shuster left the family farm at sixteen to become a clerk in Fry's General Store near Delmont, Pennsylvania. He saved his money and eventually was able to open his own general store in the new town of Monessen, about thirty miles south of Pittsburgh. Through the years he prospered, sending my father to the best private schools, building a beautiful home, and traveling extensively. He plowed his profits back into his business and mortgaged his home to raise capital for even further expansion. But when the financial panic of 1919 hit following World War I, he was wiped out—house and all. The timing was particularly bad because he became ill, and within a year, he died a broken man. He was a wonderful person and a beloved community leader, but he had made the fatal mistake of overextending himself financially. He had not diversified, had not set aside a portion of his substantial assets in secure investments. I'm sure the pain that experience caused my family left me a more cautious person where money is concerned and I hope you will learn from it, too.

Business decisions should be made based on sound business principles. Small business owners, especially, sometimes become so emotionally attached to their businesses that they make irrational decisions, pouring their life's savings into an irretrievably failing enterprise. It's hard to pull the plug on a business you consider your baby, but if you rely on your emotions rather than on sound judgment, you may be needlessly inflicting pain on both yourself and those you love.

A corollary is: buy sound stocks, but seldom sell. I made a mistake early on thinking I could study the stock market and then outsmart it. After I lost money that way, I realized that some bright people work their whole lives on Wall Street and specialize in making sophisticated judgments. It was foolish of me to second-guess the pros. Don't kid yourself into thinking you have the necessary knowledge. Rely on responsible experts instead. And invest, rather than speculate, in diversified Blue Chip stocks, as well as conservative mutual funds and municipal bonds. I don't need to waste my time pouring over daily stock quotations, making relatively uninformed decisions. And do not rely blindly on a broker. Remember, a broker is a salesman who makes his money by buying and selling stocks for you. The more he "churns" your account, the more money he makes. As a New York investor friend has told me, "Never forget the stock market was created for the benefit of the sellers, not the buyers." Another mistake I made over the years was relying on stock tips from well-intentioned friends. On balance, I've lost more money on tips than I've made. There's a human element of greed in thinking you can make an easy buck. Resist it. I wish I had. (An exception to these guidelines is my policy to invest in companies with whom I have a business relationship, as a matter of loyalty.)

As Americans, we have good reason to plan for a bright future. No people in recorded history have enjoyed the freedom and prosperity we have experienced during the past half-century. And today, America stands preeminent in the world. It's easy to assume that hard times will never return. But history teaches that *everything* in life is temporary.

To show how much the world has changed in my lifetime, consider the headlines on the front page of the *New York Herald Tribune* on Saturday, January 23, 1932—the date of my birth:

France threatens Germany.
Japanese threaten Shanghai.
Bronx women battle police with stones, singing Communist songs.
Soviets devote five-year plan to raising living standards.
NY Charity requires two days' work for $12 of food.

While we must live our lives confidently, it is only prudent to think through what we would do if adversity strikes. Economic collapse, natural disasters, or terrorism could destabilize or even destroy much of America. While the world is a dangerous place, America always has been protected by its abundance and two oceans. But that's no longer true. Weapons of mass destruction in the hands of rogue states or terrorists have created new vulnerabilities. While our nation is confronting terrorism abroad and working to provide security at home, individuals and families also must begin to think the unthinkable. How can we best survive personal adversity—or even a doomsday scenario?

Everyone should think about establishing a safe haven for their loved ones in time of emergency. By knowing there is a place on earth where you can go, even in the darkest days, you can be more secure in going about your daily life, positively planning for your future.

Shuster Lodge is my answer to that question. Although the farm has been a place for joyous occasions, and, since we bought it in 1964, a refuge to which family members can return temporarily in times of personal crisis, it also is a safe haven for the family should disaster strike; a stronghold for survival in cataclysmic times.

God forbid that America ever should be devastated, but if that dreadful day comes, the farm provides the essential elements for survival. It is reachable within a few hours from our children's homes by car and within a couple of days on foot should transportation be disrupted. A generator can provide electricity for several days and an abundant supply of wood can fuel the fireplaces indefinitely. Pure water gushes from the springs, and our stock of food can be replenished by fish from the river, wildlife from the woods, and black walnuts from along the riverbanks, until new crops can be harvested. A dairy cow can be obtained from a nearby farmer, and the horses could be used for limited transportation and garden plowing.

Should mobs pour out of the cities, scavenging the countryside, we have ample means to protect our lives and property, if that heart-wrenching necessity arises. It is difficult even to think these thoughts, but being prepared for a disaster can be the difference between life and death. Literally! Under cataclysmic circumstances, saving can refer not only to our standard of living, but to life itself.

Saving means *preserving*, and by becoming financially secure, you can help preserve the legacy we have created—a legacy that you can help pass along to future generations.

Shuster Lodge

Chapter Nine

Protecting

> *Those who expect to reap the blessings of freedom*
> *must undergo the fatigue of supporting it.*
> —Thomas Paine

Lt. James J. Murphy of Pennsylvania is one of the 10,489 Americans buried at St. Avold's in Alsace-Lorraine, France, the largest U.S. military cemetery outside the United States. He was killed on May 6, 1945, while assaulting a German infantry position. As I stood alone at his grave in the twilight of a summer evening a few years ago, I reflected that we would not be free today but for the sacrifice of soldiers like Lieutenant Murphy.

All our efforts to make the most of our lives could go for naught if America does not remain free and secure.

From the Revolutionary War through the 2003 conflict in Iraq, more than a million Americans have died defending our freedom. Imagine how different America would be under the heel of Adolf Hitler, Osama Bin Laden, or Saddam Hussein.

History has proven that war is nearly always with us. Of 3,500 years of recorded history, the world has been totally at peace for less than 300 years. Sadly, the twentieth century was the most brutal. Over 120 million people died in 130 wars—more than all those killed in all the wars in previous centuries combined. And rather than protecting them, governments have murdered 170 million of their own citizens, according to Professor R. J. Rummel in his book, *Death by Government*. The top murderers were the Soviet Union, Red China, Nazi Germany, Cambodia's Khmer Rouge, and Saddam Hussein's Iraq, together totaling more than 120 million.

What does all this have to do with us? It's our nature to recoil from these gruesome facts, and many people refuse to believe that such atrocities could ever happen again. But it's important to understand the world in which we live. It's not only a world in which we Americans have extraordinary prosperity, unprecedented opportunities, and unparalleled freedom, but also a dangerous world in which our very way of life and life itself are threatened.

The 1993 bombing of the World Trade Center in New York, the subsequent 9/11 attack on it and the Pentagon, killing nearly three thousand people, the failed attempts to blow up an Ohio shopping mall and the Brooklyn Bridge, the anthrax murders in Florida and Washington, D.C., and the beheading of innocent Americans in Afghanistan, Iraq, and Saudi Arabia, all chillingly demonstrate the fanatical determination of Islamic terrorists to cripple, if not destroy, our civilization. According to the September 11 Commission, terrorists also had plans to attack the U.S. Capitol, CIA, FBI, nuclear power plants, and buildings in California and Washington State. And the Center for Nonproliferation Studies reported that terrorists are "all but certain" to set off radiological weapons, known as "dirty bombs," in the United States, which could make cities uninhabitable for years.

Vaclav Havel, the heroic former president of the Czech Republic, has written that the North Korean dictator, Kim Jong II, is developing weapons of mass destruction and "is able to blackmail the world with the help of his huge army, nuclear weapons, long-range missiles, and the export of weaponry and military technology to like-minded dictators around the world."

Iran's ayatollahs have openly stated that they are developing nuclear capability. According to their foreign minister, Kamal Kharrazi, "This is an irreversible path."

We are at war, and if we are to preserve freedom, we cannot back away from the difficult challenges to keep America strong. Each of us has a role—large or small—to protect and support those institutions that foster a free and responsible society and to vigorously oppose those that don't.

During my life, I've seen first-hand the horrors of war, and had the opportunity to examine the mind-set of those who would destroy democracy. Through my experience as a counterintelligence agent and as the ranking member of the U.S. House Select Committee on Intelligence, I have also seen people willing to throw it all away.

At the end of the Korean War in the 1950s, I helped investigate the actions of American POWs who defected to North Korea. They had traded loyalty to their country and to their buddies for better food, shelter, and cigarettes to avoid the brutal living conditions imposed on POWs in clear violation of the Geneva Convention's code of conduct for treating prisoners. (Thirty-nine percent of the 2,806 American POWs died in the North Korean prison camps!) Eventually, twenty of the traitors were brought back to the U.S. for courts-martial.

Following that assignment, going by the undercover name George Saunders, I was put in charge of a domestic intelligence operation tracking the activities of the Communist Party in the Middle-Atlantic States. I observed American Communists following orders from Moscow to foment hatred against the U.S. among labor unions, minorities, and on college campuses in an effort to destabilize our country.

I was recruited by an elegant, wealthy woman, who publicly was considered a liberal activist, but who was known by us to be a committed Communist. We had several meetings during which she urged me to distribute Communist literature on college campuses and to look for potential recruits to "our" cause. Ironically, her freedom of speech was protected by the very Constitution she was working to subvert.

Such Moscow-directed activities were occurring across America. But far more serious were spies like Klaus Fuchs and Julius and Ethel Rosenberg, who turned over some of America's most vital secrets to the Soviets, enabling them to accelerate the development of their own atomic bomb. Since the demise of the Soviet Union, files have been opened to show how widespread their Cold War activity was against America.

Our strategy was to contain Communism by supporting our allies in regions the Soviets were attempting to dominate. Frederick the Great of Prussia, in his Seven Years War against Russia described his policy as a "strategy of exhaustion." Two hundred-fifty years later, the West, led by America, followed a similar strategy, making Soviet expansionism so costly that it ultimately contributed to the demise of an already failing economic system.

As the ranking member of the Select Intelligence Committee I was immersed in national security decisions during the Soviet Union's dissolution in 1991. My position made me a member of the "Gang of Eight"—the eight members of the House and Senate, including the House Speaker and the Senate majority leader—who, by law, were to be kept fully informed by the White House of the nation's most sensitive intelligence activities. More than any of my other congressional responsibilities, these top-secret briefings left me drained because any slip could put at risk both U.S. national security and the lives of our foreign agents. I needed a good run to clear my head. Reflecting on our intelligence accomplishments, such as our support for the Afghans against the Soviet invaders, usually gave me a lift.

That effort fit our containment policy but sometimes we made a mistake by assuming that our allies shared our democratic values. Actually, the mujahideen—Muslim warriors engaged in a jihad, a holy war—despised democracy. They were using us just as we were using them. Our national security sometimes requires doing business with barbaric people. Often, our relationships were described best by the Arab saying, "The enemy of my enemy is my friend." It turns out that by arming the Afghan mujahideen against the Soviets we provided arms that later fell into the hands of people supporting terrorists. Even though that occurred, the strategic success of hastening the demise of the Soviet Union outweighs the negative consequences.

One meeting I participated in with the mujahideen commanders in a bunker at the Kyber Pass during the war enabled me to understand their mind-set. As they pointed to maps describing the various battles taking place, I asked about their long-term strategy for ending the war, for driving the Soviet army out of Afghanistan.

They looked at me quizzically, and one of them replied, "Long-term strategy? Kill Russians."

Meeting brutality with brutality was understandable considering that the Soviets killed over a million Afghans in a country of only 18 million and maimed thousands more. We saw children whose hands had been blown off by innocently picking up small "butterfly" mines scattered on the ground by the Soviets. We saw legless boys hobbling on crude crutches. Standing nearby, a British photojournalist covering the war heatedly told me, "You go back and tell the American people that they live in heaven compared to much of the world!"

One day after we got home, a humanitarian organization brought a group of crippled Afghan children to my office to thank us for arranging medical treatment for them in the United States. One five-year-old girl's head was totally bald and badly blistered. Soviet soldiers had poured lye on her head after capturing her father. We took the group, which included a fifteen-year-old boy whose arms had been blown off at the elbows, to lunch in the House cafeteria. I motioned for one of my staff to help get him his food, but a bearded, fearsome-looking mujahideen warrior immediately stopped her. He explained through an interpreter that the boy considered himself a young mujahideen and that it would be a sign of weakness for him to be helped, especially by a woman. The warrior filled the boy's plate with French fries, the boy lowered his face down to the plate, and pushed the fries into his mouth with the stubs of his arms.

Besides the war in Afghanistan, the Soviet Union, in their quest for world domination, propped up many client states during the Cold War period. In Angola, their puppet government was opposed by Jonas Savimbi's UNITA tribes, whom we supported. In the 1980s, Cuba sent 57,000 troops as Soviet proxies to help the government fight Savimbi's guerillas.

To assure Savimbi of continued U.S. support and assess his capabilities to win the war, Congressman Bob McEwen of Ohio and I, along with Intelligence Committee staff, journeyed to his guerilla camp in the jungle of southeast Angola. Flying low to avoid enemy radar in an unmarked CIA plane at dusk, I felt like we were heading into a black hole. Suddenly, oil drums flamed with kerosene along both sides of a dirt runway. As our plane touched down, the fires in the drums were extinguished, leaving us in the immense blackness of an African night. Hustled silently into a waiting Land Rover and driven into the heart of the guerilla camp, we were ushered into Savimbi's thatched-roofed hut where we sat on mats and ate antelope and maize for dinner. We were then led to an open-air stockade and up a pair of stairs onto a wooden platform. Suddenly, torches flared and we were facing hundreds of Savimbi's stoney-faced, bandoleered fighters. I thought to myself, "I sure hope they know we're friendlies!"

One of the guerilla leaders spoke, apparently explaining who we were, and the warriors responded by thrusting their rifles in the air and repeatedly shouting, "Savimbi! Savimbi!" Through an interpreter I assured them of U.S. support in the cause of fighting the Soviet-backed forces. When I finished, I received another guns-in-the-air round of shouts.

The next morning, we were briefed on how they were going to drive out the Communists and create a democratic government headed by Savimbi's Ovimbundu tribe. With an AK-47 in hand, I had my picture taken with three of his top lieutenants. A few months later, when I was hanging the picture in my office and sought to identify them by name, I was casually informed by Savimbi's Washington spokesman that two of them had shown disloyalty and had been "eliminated."

The war dragged on for several years. When the Soviet Union collapsed, we no longer had a strategic interest in supporting Savimbi. Eventually, UNITA was defeated by Angolan government forces, and he was killed in 2002. Although Angola, along with most of Africa, remains in turmoil today, the war advanced our goal of weakening the Soviet Union.

We were more successful in Central America where our support for anti-Communist forces helped defeat Communist governments and establish democracies—although the Iran-Contra scandal (selling arms for money to support the anti-Communist Contras) caused major problems for the Reagan administration.

Cuba served as a proxy for the Soviet Union, supporting the Communist Sandinistas against the Contras in Nicaragua. We helicoptered into the jungle to assure the Contra leaders of U.S. support. The legendary Commandante Zero presented me with a machete that had been used in battles, which I keep sheathed in the back of the farm jeep to kill snakes and hack open our path on the family's annual boundary walk.

The war dragged on for several years as the Democratic Congress vacillated in its support for the Contras. While Jimmy Carter was president, Fidel Castro told our U.S. ambassador that he "would do nothing against Carter in an election year," fueling the argument that liberal Democrats were soft on Communism.

After the election of Ronald Reagan, our stepped-up aid to the Contras and the Cuban loss of Soviet support as the superpower imploded forced the Sandinistas to agree to free elections. They were badly defeated by Violeta Chamorro, a widow whose husband, Pedro, the publisher of *La Prensa* newspaper, had been murdered by the Sandinistas. Nicaragua is a democracy today.

At the same time, in nearby El Salvador, a civil war raged between the democratically elected government and the Farabundo Marti National Liberation Front (FMLN) Communists. On an Intelligence Committee sweep through Central America, I witnessed the interrogation of an FMLN terrorist who had just been captured attempting to blow up a hotel and was being held in a Salvadoran prison. We previously had confronted Nicaragua's foreign minister, a suspended Catholic priest, who denied that his government supported the Communist terrorists in El Salvador, even though his own president, Daniel Ortega, had bragged about it. Despite the lies and distortions of the Sandinistas and FMLN Communists, their propaganda was swallowed by much of the left around the world. The

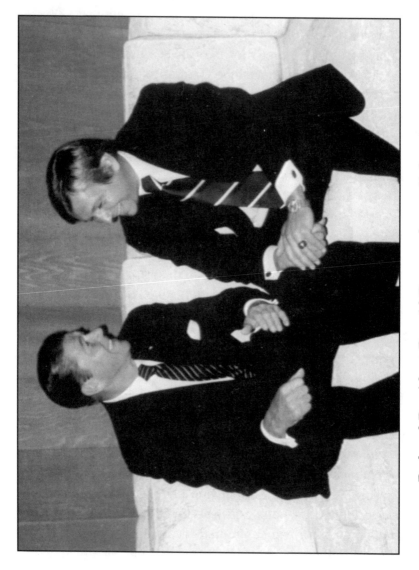

Bud and President Ronald Reagan share a light moment

same was true in America, too, undermining U.S. efforts to stop the spread of Marxist revolutions in our hemisphere. Lenin's guidance to Feliks Dzerhinsky, the founder of the Soviet intelligence system, still rings true today in many quarters: "The West are wishful thinkers, so we will give them what they want to think."

I, perhaps, had been a "wishful thinker," initially believing that only the Communists were the bad guys. In 1989, a year after our first trip to El Salvador, FMLN guerillas attacked the capital, San Salvador, killing over a thousand soldiers and hundreds of civilians. It was widely believed that Jesuit priests, who had openly advocated a Marxist government, had instigated the bloody siege. Five days later, six Jesuit priests, their cook, and her fifteen-year-old daughter were murdered at a nearby university. The world was shocked, and the U.S. Congress, which supported the Salvadoran government with millions in foreign aid, demanded an investigation.

Congressman Joe Moakley, a Massachusetts Democrat, and I were tapped to lead a bipartisan investigation. I was ready to accept the Salvadoran government's claims that they would vigorously investigate the murders of the priests, which were thought to have been carried out by rogue, right-wing, Army death squads. But our team conducted an extensive investigation, interviewing a number of people both in and out of government. Reluctantly, I concluded that the military was covering up, not investigating, the crime. Not a single Army officer came forward to cooperate. We were being stonewalled.

When we returned to Washington, Congressman Moakley and I issued a blistering report condemning both the FMLN for their attacks, and the Army for its apparent cover-up. I came away from the experience feeling that in bitter conflicts there aren't any completely good guys. Once again, based on geopolitical necessity, we were dealing with undemocratic forces—the lesser of two evils—to support a broader strategic goal. But I developed a deep respect for Joe Moakley's patriotism, even though we were politically far apart. (I was pleased that I was able to move through our committee the naming of the Boston courthouse in his honor before his untimely death from cancer in 2001.)

In March 1989, after returning from an intelligence trip to Panama, I inserted a report in the *Congressional Record* calling for the removal of General Manuel Noriega. U.S. access to the canal was threatened by Cuban, Libyan, and Nicaraguan efforts to prop up the dictator. Eight months later, the U.S. invaded Panama, removing Noriega and returning the country to civilian control.

Through our painful and costly efforts to support democracy in Central America, Castro's goal of using the region as a stepping-stone to Mexico and America's borders was denied. While our relationships south of the border are far from perfect, the menace of Communist dictatorships no longer exists, thanks to our resolve, as well as to the failure of Marxist economics.

The weaknesses of Communism were never made clearer than by comparing the difference between West and East Berlin during the Cold War—same city, same people, same country. The only difference was that West Berlin was part of the democratic, market economy of the Western alliance, and East Berlin was behind the Iron Curtain—part of the Communist satellite system controlled by the Soviet Union.

Passing through the Berlin Wall at "Checkpoint Charlie" from West Berlin into East Berlin—a distance of perhaps fifty yards—as I did in 1988, we went from a clean, vibrant, prosperous society into a dull, decaying, backward world. A few plainly clad folks shuffled through the dirty, nearly empty streets beside a 1950s vintage streetcar slowly clanking along.

Our U.S. military escort drove us to the building where German generals had signed surrender documents at the end of World War II. To our surprise, Soviet, rather than East German soldiers, guarded the building, which an Army captain refused to let us enter. As we stood on tiptoe at a window straining to see, our military escort took the Soviet officer aside and whispered to him. He strolled over to his guard shack while our escort retrieved a brown paper bag from our van and left it on the floor inside the shack. The captain unlocked the door to the building, and we were able to walk into the room and touch the table where history had been made.

As we passed back into West Berlin through "Checkpoint Charlie," I asked our escort what he had given the guard in the paper bag.

"A six-pack of Pepsi Cola," he replied. "They can't get soft drinks in East Berlin." So much for the wonderful world of Communism!

Soon after the Cold War ended, we faced a different kind of threat. Members of the Intelligence Committee were shown clear evidence that Saddam Hussein's objective was not simply to invade Kuwait, but rather to march through it to Saudi Arabia, Bahrain, Qatar, and on to the Gulf of Oman, ultimately gaining control of 70 percent of the world's oil.

I will always be grateful for the role I was able to play in that war. I had previously authored a classified project, code named "Robin Quart," to use low-flying intelligence-gathering planes to go after Columbian drug lords. ("Robin Quart" was instrumental in bringing down leaders of the Cali drug cartel.)

As staging for the Gulf war began, the planes were moved to Bahrain. Hours before the ground war started, "Robin Quart" planes crossed the border into Iraq, located several Iraqi military command and control forward posts, and down-linked the intelligence to the "Robin Quart" soldiers on the ground. Our soldiers attacked, destroying several important Iraqi command posts, before returning across the border, having suffered no casualties.

After the war, soldiers from "Robin Quart" came to my office and presented to me a captured Iraqi battle flag with an inscription thanking me for "unparalleled, dedicated, and sincere support. The result of your untiring efforts is a truly significant national intelligence capability."

I also had the privilege of playing a role in feeding disinformation to the Iraqis prior to the start of the war. As we met with U.S. commanders aboard the USS *LaSalle*, one of General Norman Schwarzkopf's officers approached me: "Congressman, I believe you were a counterintelligence agent toward the end of the Korean war. When we go topside after this briefing, the Iraqis will be watching the press conference. Would you be willing to say that based on the briefing you have just received, our invasion is going to surpass MacArthur's historic amphibious landing at Inch'on?"

"I'd be happy to," I replied, and a few minutes later, on the deck of the USS *LaSalle*, I energetically described the "briefing."

When the ground war began, the U.S. conspicuously anchored a ship with Marines off the eastern coast of Iraq, Saddam moved 20,000 troops eastward to defend against the expected amphibious landing, and the U.S. Army swept westward around his flank to achieve a stunning 100-hour victory. (There's no way to measure the effect of my pressconference ploy, but I still smile every time I think of it.)

Later, in classified briefings by the administration, I expressed my strong opposition to halting the war when we did. My judgment then (and now) was that we made an epic error by not removing Saddam from power. There were diplomatic reasons for stopping when we did—the risk of losing the support of our Arab allies—and I respect former President Bush and his advisors. But I believe the decision they made was incorrect. Indeed, we were assured by the administration that Saddam "would be gone within a year—overthrown by his own people." To paraphrase Machiavelli, "Never wound a despot. Destroy him." The world would be a much safer place today had we changed the Iraqi regime in 1991 rather than waiting until 2003.

Americans are understandably focused on the immediate terrorist threats, but it also is important to recognize the long-term strategic implications of other global trends, and how they can affect our lives in the coming decades. Nationwide, the Census Bureau projects a population increase from 286 million to 325 million by 2020. Energy consumption is projected to increase by 44 percent in the next thirty years. It will become even more prudent to practice conservation, explore alternative forms of energy, and vigorously support efforts to increase domestic production. U.S. production of nuclear and hydroelectric power will decline due to government mandates. While coal is our most abundant source of energy, it produces only about 20 percent of the nation's supply, and is in danger of being further curtailed by environmental regulations, however well intended. Heavy demand for natural gas will drive up prices even more, which already have doubled in the past decade.

California's late 1990s energy crisis may well be a harbinger of things to come for the nation. The Golden State's energy demand in the past fifteen years has increased by more than twice the national average. It produces less energy per capita than any other state, has not built a new power plant in over a dozen years, has banned coal-generating facilities, and, by deregulating wholesale prices of electricity while keeping a cap on retail prices, has plunged its power companies into insolvency. Brownouts are frequent, and blackouts are looming.

Worldwide, population is slated to exceed 7.5 billion by 2020, a 41 percent increase in thirty years, with most of the growth occurring in underdeveloped countries. Global demand for energy will soar over 50 percent according to the Center for Strategic and International Studies.

Napoleon observed, "When China awakes, the earth will shake." With over a billion people and a modernization program that already is producing double-digit economic growth annually, China is more than stirring. She is catapulting forward to become one of the world's great competitors in this new century. By 2020, China will have 14 percent of the international trade, surpassing the U.S.'s 11 percent. Whether she chooses to develop the military capacity to dominate the Far East and even challenge the West, is an open question. But, we must be prepared to compete with China in the marketplace and to protect America against her if she becomes aggressively militaristic. Her growing demand for energy resources surely will place added pressure on world demand for energy. Most forecasters see no major breakthroughs for new energy sources. The Persian Gulf will remain the largest supplier of oil, but the region would have to increase production by 80 percent to meet world demand, a highly unlikely, if not impossible, scenario.

U.S. and world demand for limited energy resources, much of which is located in the volatile Middle East, could lead to energy wars, exacerbated by poverty and terrorism. Such wars could cause economic chaos—deep recessions or even long-term economic stagnation—crippling our lifestyles.

In the coming years, over 3 billion people in third-world countries will face serious water shortages, increasing the potential for famine, according to the National Foreign Intelligence Board: "Regions, countries and groups feeling left behind will face deepening economic stagnation, political instability, and cultural alienation."

Terrorist organizations from around the world already have declared a jihad against the United States. In the three years following 9/11, over twenty major terrorist attacks have occurred against American interests worldwide. James Woolsey, former director of the CIA, stated: "Today's terrorists don't want a seat at the table. They want to destroy the table and everyone sitting at it." To compound the problem, the development and accessibility to weapons of mass destruction means that future terror strikes could dwarf the horrors of 9/11. Warren Buffett, a wise man, who is the second richest in America and has made billions by accurately predicting the future, recently said: "It is virtually a 100 percent certainty that America will be struck by a nuclear weapon. Not *if*, but *when*."

What do these dire predictions, coupled with the terrorist attacks we have already experienced, mean for the future? If we face the evidence squarely, we will realize that we have entered a twilight zone of trouble—an "age of terrorism"—that may be with us for a lifetime. Yet there is nothing to be gained by wringing our hands and waiting helplessly for a doomsday that may never come.

Rather, we can live our lives positively and productively, understanding the dangerous world in which we live, and resolving to be good citizens. We can commit our energies to supporting efforts to protect America, to keeping her strong. One does not have to become a national leader to make an impact. We can become involved in local, state, and national activities to build and strengthen our community, charitable, and professional organizations. There are many worthy areas in which to work.

We can remember the harsh lesson of history that strength deters aggression, weakness invites it. Alexander Solzhenitsyn, the great Russian writer, in his 1970 Nobel lecture, referring to British Prime Minister Neville Chamberlain's capitulation to Hitler at Munich, said: "The Spirit of Munich is a disease of the will of prosperous people...the intimidated civilized world has found nothing to oppose the onslaught of a suddenly resurgent fang-baring barbarism, except concessions and smiles."

There are, indeed, people in America and around the world who oppose maintaining a strong national defense, who, in the words of Rodney King, whose arrest instigated the 1992 Los Angeles riots, ask, "Why can't we all just get along?" How wonderful it would be if it were that simple. We must resist the siren call of those who think peace can be achieved in the world by being nice to our enemies. In fact, many of the so-called peace movements in the world were actually organized by our enemies to weaken our resolve. During the Cold War, payments for "peace" ads in the Denmark newspapers were traced to the Soviet Embassy. Napoleon's dictum, "Talk peace and think war," is still practiced today in many parts of the world, including the Middle East.

Of course, we want to get along with our neighbors and our allies, but we need to understand that there is evil in the world—people, organizations, and governments who want to destroy America and kill us! We have a duty to ourselves, our families, and our posterity to keep America strong—to play our individual roles, however large or small, to help protect America.

During my service in Congress, part of my morning ritual was to repeat my Oath of Office to myself. Having done it for so many years, I discovered upon my retirement that it continued to flow naturally through my head following my morning prayers. It struck me that one doesn't have to be a U.S. congressman for the words to have meaning. So, as a private citizen of this great land, I still recite it, slightly revised, to myself each morning:

> *I do solemnly swear that I will support and defend the Constitution of the United States against all enemies, foreign and domestic; that I will bear true faith and allegiance to the same; that I take this obligation freely, without any*

mental reservation or purpose of evasion, and that I will
well and faithfully discharge my duties as a private citizen.
So help me God.

Remembering the proudest boast of Roman citizens two thousand years ago, "Civis Romanus Sum"—I am a Roman citizen—I add: *"I am an American citizen!"*

As we go through life, we should never forget the extraordinary privilege of being an American citizen.

We should never forget that if we ever value anything more than freedom, eventually we not only will lose our freedom but that which we have placed above it.

Chapter Ten
Bonding

Family is forever.

--Anonymous

When Gwyneth Paltrow accepted her Oscar for Best Actress in *Shakespeare in Love* a few years ago, she said, "You can go far when your parents really love you!"

What a blessing it is to be nurtured as a child by a loving family. The bonds that embrace us, protect us, and encourage us can almost never be completely broken—though they sometimes can be tattered or strained. Even if we sever our ties, our family still influences who we are.

We are connected to the generations that came before us. The blood of German, Scotch, English, Irish, Italian, Jewish, and American Indian ancestors flows through the veins of our twelve grandchildren. But more than our ancestors' genetic makeup, we inherit their values and culture, their happiness and heartaches, and many of their unfulfilled dreams. Similarly, those who follow us will be blessed—or burdened—by what we pass on to them.

The first book I remember reading as a youngster (with my mother's help) was *The Five Little Bunkers*, a story about a loving family with five children. When my children were young, I often drew on it to tell a story called "The Five Little Shusters and How They Came To Be"—a simplified version of how they ended up on this earth, in America, in Pennsylvania, during the second half of the twentieth century. This is how the story goes:

It was the turn of the century, and Major Robert Lyon, the former mayor of Pittsburgh and a decorated Civil War veteran, rocked contentedly on his front porch in the shadow of Forbes Field, home of the Pittsburgh Pirates, while his baby granddaughter, "Bunny," cooed in a nearby bassinet. Reading of Teddy Roosevelt's recent charge up San Juan Hill, he felt a tinge of pride over his own decoration for "conspicuous gallantry" in the battle of Cold Harbor, Virginia, where he was seriously wounded, and the role his great-grandfather, John Lyon, had played as one of George Washington's Quartermasters during the Revolutionary War.

Fourteen miles upriver, on the eastern bank of the Monongahela River, Elmer Greinert pinned a barber's sheet around the neck of a craftsman from the local glass factory, known as the Glass House. Dipping a shaving brush into one of the hand-painted mugs he kept in cubbyholes in a rack on the wall, he lathered his customer. Like all the others in the rack, the mug was decorated by Greinert's wife, Pearl Hart. On it, surrounded by delicately painted flowers, was the finely inscrolled name of Harry Rommel.

The young barber and the glassmaker, both of German stock, talked about the coming Sunday when they planned to help lay out lots in their newly incorporated town, Glassport, and about their children, Grace Greinert and Frank Rommel. Rommel was thrilled that, after three daughters whom he loved dearly, he now had a son to carry on the family name. For Greinert, Grace was his only child— she had been adopted when her mother, Pearl's sister, had died— and he doted on her.

Rommel's grandfather, Heinrich, had been an officer in an elite cavalry unit in Germany, the Cuirassiers, but when his superiors denied his request to marry his sweetheart, Mary Dicker, because she was a Catholic, he resigned his commission and they immigrated to the United States.

Greinert's father, a glassmaker, had left Germany to avoid fighting in one of Otto Von Bismarck's wars to unify Germany.

Fourteen miles upriver from Glassport, another town, called Monessen, was springing up. The townspeople there had just elected a farm-boy-turned-grocer, Alpheus Shuster, as their mayor (or burgess, as they called it then). He, too, was thinking about the new town he was helping to build with his pretty wife, Bess, and their newborn son, Prather, whom they nicknamed "Pat."

Al could have been growing up in the Rhine, rather than the Mon, Valley, had it not been for his ancestors, Garrett Shuster, his great-great-grandfather, and Michael Kepple, his great-great-great-grandfather, the son of the schoolmaster in Herbitzheim, Germany. Their families had joined the great exodus in the 1750s of some 50,000 Germans to Pennsylvania in search of religious freedom and fertile farmland. They came to be called the "Pennsylvania Deutsch," which eventually was anglicized to "Pennsylvania Dutch."

Michael Kepple served as a scout for Colonel Henri Bouquet, who defeated Kyashuta, chief of the Senecas, in the 1763 Battle of Bushy Run in western Pennsylvania. His defeat ended the Indian uprising, opening the land west of the Allegheny Mountains for settlement. During the battle, Bouquet sent Kepple on a dangerous mission to seek reinforcements from Fort Pitt, twenty miles away. En route, he was captured by Indians. Kepple was released at Fort Pitt only after the hostilities ended the following year. But that wasn't the end of his Indian troubles.

In a raid a few years later, Kepple's eighteen-month-old granddaughter, Dorothea, was captured and taken to Massena, New York. The family history passed down a century ago by Uncle Peter Kepple, my great-grandmother's brother, has it that the Indians did not kill her, as was their usual custom with infants (by swinging them by their feet and smashing their heads into a tree), because they were fascinated by her blonde hair. A French trapper saw baby Dorothea in the Indian camp, crept in at night, slashed the throat of a puppy sleeping with her to keep it from barking, and dragged the lifeless, bleeding dog along the river bank to create a false trail. He then hid the baby under furs in his canoe, eventually reaching Fort Niagara where she was turned over to the British, and finally united with her family at Fort Pitt. (Dorothea was my great-great-great-great-grandmother.)

The Shusters and the Kepples intermarried, making me a descendant of two of Michael Kepple's sons, Andrew and Nickolas. When the Shusters and the Kepples crossed the Allegheny Mountains in the 1770s, and the Rommels and the Greinerts followed their glassmaking trade to the shores of the Monongahela River (which later became the Steel Valley) around 1900, they had no way of knowing that their lives would intersect.

As Al Shuster's general store prospered, he expanded his business interests into real estate and insurance. He also built the valley's first opera house with a stage for live performances and a screen for silent movies. His friends teased him that the real reason he built the theater was so that his son, Pat, a talented baritone, could entertain at intermission. When Pat got a little older, Al and Bess proudly sent him off to prep school and then to Staunton Military Academy in Virginia.

But within a few years, Al's growing prosperity was crushed by the financial panic following World War I, a fate exacerbated by his unwillingness to cut off credit to families who couldn't pay their bills. When he died not long after, the cars literally lined the street from the church to the cemetery. Though I never knew my Grandfather Shuster, he was larger than life for me, an example of how a person should live—working, producing, building, and caring. His memory is an important reminder that we can touch the lives of people we have never met.

Beloved as his father was, his financial collapse sent his son, Pat, scurrying for work, eventually taking him to a steel mill across the river from the Glass House. He met the barber's daughter, Grace Greinert, at a local party and married her. Six years later, in the depths of the Great Depression, a son was born whom they named after her father.

Around the same time, Frank Rommel was introduced to "Bunny" Lyon at a church social. They, too, were married and eventually had a daughter: Harriett Patricia Rommel.

Several years later, on a warm fall day in 1945, soon after Harry Truman had ended World War II by dropping two history-making atomic bombs on Japan, the ninth-grade homeroom teacher at

Glassport High School assigned students alphabetically to their seats, thereby making a little history of her own. Shuster sat behind Rommel, and that was the beginning of how, many years later, the five little Shusters came to be.

In every family there are good times and bad. Mine was no exception. The Great Depression and World War II, which broke millions of hearts and homes around the world, diverted my father away from completing his education and realizing his talent as a musician.

He had a strong, pure voice and could play nearly anything on the piano effortlessly. One Saturday afternoon after pressing his ear to the radio to hear the New York Philharmonic play the Overture by Franz von Suppe from *The Poet and the Peasant*, he sat down at our out-of-tune piano and, stumbling through the music just once, went on to play it almost perfectly. He also got great joy out of reciting long passages from Longfellow and Shakespeare. Full of energy, he loved my mother fiercely and didn't know how to be mean to anyone. Years later, one of my older boyhood friends told me, "Your dad wasn't the life of the party...he was the *whole* party!"

But he also didn't know how to make a dime. He often was out of work, causing us to rely on my Greinert grandparents, who doted on both my mother and me. I kept a log during my Army days, and wrote the following entry on February 25, 1955, soon after my twenty-third birthday:

> My father barely pulled through a serious operation, the effects of which, along with his acute worry over being out of work for the past several months and in debt, has caused his near-collapse. I am now responsible for the household. My future is highly questionable. In the midst of all this trouble and worry, I find that one intense belief remains—the belief that I can succeed and carve a place for myself in society. I pray that such an attitude is not sinful. If it were not for God, my country, friends and loved ones, I would nurture no such thoughts. I pray I may succeed and never forget these trying days.

Though my dad finally went back to work, he was a shell of the man he had been. His failures gnawed deeply at him, and he repeatedly emphasized to me, "You're like your grandfather Shuster, but I guess his abilities skipped a generation. They passed me by."

With my dad back on the payroll and my own career progressing nicely, I thought the family crisis was behind us. But about a year later, in 1957, my mother was rushed to the hospital with an embolism blocking the blood to the arteries in both legs. The doctors misdiagnosed the illness as pneumonia, but my brother-in-law, Dr. Frank Rommel, who was interning there, caught the problem, probably saving her life. She was moved to a hospital in Pittsburgh where she went through an agonizing nine months of operations.

On March 14, 1971, a year after my mother died, I wrote a letter to my children describing her ordeal, which I filed away for the future:

My dear children,

You must never forget the story of "Gay," your grandmother. Thirteen years before she died, she was hospitalized and suffered a nine-month ordeal. She had to have both her legs amputated to save her life from a blood clot, as well as a mitral valve heart operation. She had nine operations because in an attempt to save as much of her legs as possible, they first amputated only above her foot. Ultimately, they amputated seven times on one leg to eliminate the poisonous gangrene. They amputated the other leg above the knee, and several weeks later performed the heart surgery.

Because she was bedfast and unable to move, she developed open sores over her body. During my lunch hour, I would go to the hospital and rub her back with cream.

The point of this story is not simply that she suffered incredibly, but rather, how she lived through it. After leaving the hospital she was bedfast for several months at home. At first, she said she didn't want to live, but the birth of our first child, Peggy, brightened her spirits and gave her something to live for.

Eventually, she was able to get around in a wheelchair, but was confined to it for the rest of her life. It is what she did with that life that makes this the story of a gallant woman.

After her tragedy, Gay was, without a doubt, one of the most cheerful, energetic, active women alive, even though she was bound to her wheelchair. She told me that she decided she could be an example for everyone around her, especially people who were suffering: "My example will say, look at me and see how cheerful I am; what a full life I live; so whatever your problem, don't feel too badly; life is good—make the most of it."

When my father became ill, we purchased a newspaper distributorship and store that my mother managed. When she became ill, the employees pitched in and kept it going until she could return. And she did—wheeling around in her chair. We lowered the counters and the cash register for her, and the customers were wonderful. We also built an addition onto the house, lowering the cupboards and widening the doors to help provide independent living.

Gay always had projects underway. She worked on knitting or crocheting for her grandchildren, and spent a year making a dress for your mother. She embroidered a map for me of the fifty states with a flower and name of each state around the border. Even more important, she had a very special project. When she heard of people who had undergone serious operations, especially amputations, she wrote to them, told them how well she was doing, and encouraged them to build a new life.

Gay had so much love in her heart that she *had* to use it encouraging other people. I'm sure when she was alone, there were tears and sadness over her plight, but we never saw them. She said, "I have only one life to live—perhaps only a few more years. I can spend them feeling sorry for myself, or I can help other people through their suffering. No matter how much my stumps ache, no matter how hard it is to move around in my chair, no one will ever know it, for by my will alone, I will rise above it. I will make my life worthwhile."

This, children, is the story of Gay, your grandmother. Before she died, the Homemakers Guild of America named her "Outstanding Woman of the Year." When she died, people came from all walks of life to pay their respects. To paraphrase Shakespeare's eulogy at Caesar's death: *Here was a woman...when shall there be another like her!*

Being at her side during those excruciating days was the least I could do, considering how she had always looked out for me. I wish I had been more considerate growing up. One Saturday evening when I was a boy, my mother took me on the "99" streetcar (from which I got the idea to name Interstate "99" in Pennsylvania) from Glassport to McKeesport to buy a pair of shoes. We found a perfectly sturdy pair for $8, but I wanted a classy pair of maroon wide-sole "spade" shoes that cost $12, even though my parents were pinching pennies in hard times. I raised such a ruckus in the crowded store that my mother finally relented and let me have my way. I wince every time I recall how inconsiderate I was. But despite my foolish behavior, her love was unconditional.

I recently came across a letter my mother wrote me on Christmas Eve, when I was seventeen:

Christmas Eve, 1949

Dearest Son,

Merry Christmas and best wishes for the New Year. I hope we can do more for you in the coming year.

Remember how I used to read the Christmas Story every Christmas Eve before you got into bed.

If caring for someone can help them get along, you should go over the top Kid, for you'll never know how much I do care for you.

Always be honorable and good.

Lots of love,
Mom

While we struggled financially, we were never lacking for love. During our troubles, our extended family also provided a cocoon. They were there for us! They cried and laughed with us, they encouraged and loved us. I had three Uncle Bills—Greinert, Shuster, and Zeigler. I'm sure I named my first son Bill because it was a very special name to me. (Even the first horse I ever rode, bareback, as a kid—a Belgian workhorse—was named Bill.) Take the time to cultivate close family ties, for they will contribute mightily to your sense of belonging.

Almost every family experiences times of heartache and fear. It's part of living. We had that kind of experience with our daughter Debbie. When she was only five, she became weak and had to be hospitalized with a high fever. But her condition deteriorated, and the doctor finally told us, "I'm afraid your little girl has acute myelogenous leukemia. If you're Catholics, I recommend she be given the last rites." Stunned, we asked if there wasn't something that could be done to save her. Another doctor said she wasn't certain of the diagnosis, and made arrangements to have her admitted to the children's cancer ward at the National Institutes of Health in Bethesda, Maryland.

Terrified, I carried her into the hospital in my arms. During the week we spent in the lounge of that ward with other grief-stricken parents, we saw bald children undergoing chemotherapy treatments and others helplessly hooked up to medical devices. It was heart wrenching.

But at the end of the week, the doctor took us aside and reported, "Your daughter does not have leukemia. She has spherocytosis—perfectly good red blood cells that are spherically shaped. When the spleen becomes infected with a virus, it reacts by mistaking them as bad cells and begins destroying them. We see this among people of German ancestry. The Amish, for example, refuse surgery for their children, and the kids die. Removal of the spleen, however, is a hundred percent cure."

We felt so relieved, so blessed, that we couldn't even face the other parents we had come to know whose children were at death's door. We quietly exited down the back stairs. Debbie's life was made whole again, enabling her to become a highly successful CPA with a loving family. Her son, Greggie, had to have the operation, and now he's energetically displaying his Shuster engine. As Winston Churchill once said, "There's nothing quite so exhilarating as having been shot at and missed."

And yet few things are sadder than unnecessary, self-inflicted wounds. Sometimes, unknowingly, we inflict pain on those we love, or those we have a duty to protect. Whether we are young or old, a lack of personal discipline, of not keeping our priorities straight, is a prescription for disaster. Controlling our passions is undoubtedly more difficult for some than for others, but that does not excuse the need for eternal wrestling with our demons—for constant self-examination and dedication to our duties.

The practical consequences of uncontrolled human weaknesses can be severe. The so-called "seven deadly sins"—pride, greed, envy, anger, lust, gluttony, sloth—affect not only our own lives but have a serious impact on our family and our friends. Anger, for example, not only gives us a negative emotional jolt, it hurts those at whom it is directed. While gluttony can destroy our health, it also inflicts emotional and financial pain on our families. Most of us are far from perfect, and I, of course, plead guilty to my share of faults. But by understanding our human weaknesses and trying to control them, we make ourselves better people and improve the lives of those we touch.

And the consequences of not practicing self-control or getting the help we need can be devastating. One of my computer managers lost his job, his family, and, ultimately, his life from alcoholism. He rented a room at the YMCA one evening and literally drank himself to death. A counterintelligence agent with whom I served became so addicted to gambling that he would sneak off to the track while he was on duty. His wife finally left him and remarried. To his deep regret, he had to watch from afar as another man raised his children. And one of my congressional colleagues left his family for a beautiful young woman who later dumped him when he lost his seat.

Though it's impossible to predict the future with any certainty, few decisions are more important than choosing one's husband or wife. Ben Franklin said, "Keep your eyes wide open before marriage, and half-shut afterwards," meaning: Be very careful in selecting the right person and then willing to overlook differences to get along.

Sometimes, young people (with hormones raging) "fall in love" with one of the first physically attractive boys or girls who pays attention to them. While personal appearance is a factor, choosing a lifetime partner deserves a more careful, thoughtful, and even somewhat unemotional evaluation. It's tough for young people to make mature decisions, yet your future depends on it.

How emotionally stable, bright, and educated is your sweetheart? What are his or her personal habits, work ethic, and core values? Is he or she affable? Ambitious? Purposeful? Try to picture life with your prospective partner, not as one continuous honeymoon, but as parents raising children together, choosing where to live, how to spend evenings at home, and who your friends will be. Consider your financial prospects, for money is often at the root of most serious arguments. Our family is blessed by the outstanding quality of our children's spouses and a close bond between my children as siblings, but every family has its disagreements. Arguments sometimes can lead to years of estrangement. I knew two brothers who couldn't agree on how to run the family roofing business handed down to them by their father. Eventually, their disagreements became so bitter that the younger brother finally formed his own company to compete against the family business. They never spoke, and their families were expected not to associate with one another. No one knew who was to blame. Perhaps both were. Family feuds do happen. Making an effort to bend and admitting that you may be partially wrong can go a long way toward mending a battered relationship. Years—or even generations—of common heritage should not be tossed aside because of one or two momentary lapses of conduct that result in bitter words or actions. Sometimes, problems can be created by loved ones who unintentionally give you bad advice based on their interest rather than yours. Listen carefully, but ultimately, only you can decide what is best for you. Remember the Latin *"Qui bono?"*—Who benefits?

The best advice parents can give their children often isn't what we say, but the example we set. Grammy has been the glue that has held our family together, and now a new generation is benefiting from her love and guidance. Her dedication has permitted me to go forth into the world to provide for the family and build an enduring legacy for us all.

Part of the legacy of our little clan is Shuster Lodge. It is much more than just a ninety-acre farm located along the Raystown branch of the Juniata River in Bedford County, Pennsylvania. It is a celebration of family and it is a refuge against life's vicissitudes. It is meant to be the one place on earth where we can return to enjoy the happiest of days or retreat in times of sorrow. By conscious design, years of effort, and a great deal of love, we have shaped it into the one place on earth where we have put down roots. All of it—the stone home, the barn, the log cabin, and the land they sit on—now belongs to our children and will be passed down to future generations. But it will be meaningful to them only if it is used, embraced, and enjoyed as a part of their lives.

We have tried to create the ambience, circumstances, and traditions that will help future generations feel the tug of these roots. In one of the stones beside the front door of Shuster Lodge is the inscription: "Dedicated to those who came before, who built so we might thrive." The initials and birth dates of our children chiseled into fireplace stones in the rec room and those of our grandchildren engraved on an adjacent stone wall are but the beginnings of generational records.

For me, the black walnut grove beside the river is my favorite spot on earth. There beside the flowing waters in the stillness of a summer day or knee-deep in snow, I have given thanks for my many blessings. And it holds special meaning because family members have been baptized there under the weathered cross, carved into a tree by our children. The keepsake Bible we've used includes stitched-in swatches of leather taken from my mother's Bible (used both by my son, Bill, and me in taking our Congressional oaths of office). We have held church services and picnics with our friends and families.

An acre in the woods facing the lane has been set aside for each grandchild, with their name on a sign in front of their acre. The family "boundary walk" around the perimeter of the farm each October, with refreshments at "Shuster Rock," and wood splitting on Thanksgiving morning, are rituals that I hope will be remembered and enjoyed long after we are gone. Shuster Cemetery, set back in the woods, will remind our descendants of those who came before and the continuity of their lives. The three pin oak saplings planted at the births of Michael, Jonathan, and Daniel will grow tall and strong as they do.

Every family needs its own unique rituals to create fond memories and shared habits.

Beyond a shared sense of place, creating memorable events can help bind family members one to another. Bill will never forget his twenty-first birthday on a twenty-degree-below-zero night in Moscow, where he accompanied me as my aide. The congressional delegation felt we should do something special to celebrate the occasion, so we chose an Azerbaijani restaurant where male musicians from

Our Shuster Family Prayer, that I wrote in 1965, and recite at
Thanksgiving and other special events, reminds us of who we are, our
many blessings, and our duties to future generations:

We give thanks for our many blessings,
For our freedom and our opportunity,
Our family and our friends,
For our feeling and being,
Our loving and knowing,
For the beauty of the earth
And the land in which we live;
For those who came before us
Who built so we may thrive...
For this mighty abundance
We are thankful,
And pledge ourselves anew
To greater strength of our minds
Our spirits and our bodies,
So we may achieve both happiness
And worthiness for ourselves
And those we touch.

Amen

the Moscow symphony also happened to be dining. When they recognized us as Americans, they sent us a round of vodka, and, of
course, in the interest of international brotherhood, we had to recip-
rocate. After much reciprocity, they decided that we should dance in
the Azerbaijani style, where men dance with men. So they grabbed
us and we whirled around the dance floor in the cause of good international relations. Finally, as midnight approached and with Bill's
birthday nearly upon us, someone in the delegation decided that to
really properly mark the auspicious occasion, we should take our
bottles of vodka and proceed to Lenin's tomb, where we would me-
morialize the event by urinating on his tomb. Our security and State
Department details tried to dissuade us, but the members of the
delegation thought it was a capital idea (over my protestations, of
course)—an act of American patriotism to express our profound contempt for Communism, and to give Bill a memory he would never
forget. We ordered them to drive us there.

With great misgivings, they pulled our embassy vans to within about fifty yards of the tomb. We piled out of the vans with bottles of vodka in hand and were trudging through two feet of snow enthusiastically shouting several unprintable words until the guards, goose-stepping in front of the tomb, spotted us. They halted, lowered their kalashnikovs, and stepped toward us. We all became instantly sober and retreated to the vans much more quickly than we had left them. We were hustled into them by our security people who sped us away in safety to our hotel. Neither Bill nor I will ever forget his twenty-first birthday!

My son Bob's trip with me to Africa, while not quite so hair-raising, will be a lifetime memory for both of us: jogging through Capetown beneath Table Mountain, descending deep into a diamond mine, cruising up the Zambezi River between hippopotamuses, and trekking past Victoria Falls to Zambia.

Strolling down the Champs Elysees in Paris with my three daughters, or waltzing with my daughter Gia at a New Year's Eve Ball in a Viennese palace, will surely be among their treasured memories—as they are among mine.

I'll never forget bursting with pride as my daughter Peggy was named the Laurel Ball Debutante at the Pennsylvania Society's 1977 Cherry Blossom Ball in Washington, D.C. Not bad, for the daughter of a boy from the Steel Valley, I thought.

Our winter family vacations in the Caribbean (all twenty-four of us!) will be remembered by our grandchildren long after they are grown and we are gone. And the "cousins' weekend" at the farm brings a new generation together.

Searching out ways to create memories is a wonderful approach to strengthen the ties that bind one unto another.

* * *

While the bonds of friendship can never truly replace family ties, they can still enrich our lives. There is an old German saying, "Ein Mensch ist kein Mensch,"—one man is no man, we need one another. We covet the companionship and the warmth of genial relationships.

True friendship is based on an emotional bond of long-standing shared experiences that have melded people's lives together, on caring and concern about the other person's well-being.

Many of my closest friends are my Sigma Chi fraternity brothers from Pitt. Even though our lives have taken us in different directions, the bonds we formed during those formative years have held us together for over half a century. Coming out of the steel valleys of Western Pennsylvania and into a great university and an exciting world filled with challenges and opportunities far beyond our parents' reach provided the foundation for our friendship. Early experiences—from "Hell Week" to a moving initiation ritual, from Monday evening meetings to weekend social events—combined to make a group of us within the fraternity true "brothers." We know each other's strengths and weaknesses, and we have shared our joys and sorrows. Although we have different temperaments, talents, and convictions, we have gained strength, even wisdom, from those very differences. Our careers include: corporate executive, small businessman, lawyer, physician, politician, teacher, author, and clergyman. We are Protestant, Catholic, agnostic, fundamentalist, liberal, and conservative. We are *very* different. Our friendships have endured and enriched our lives, not simply because of the deep bonds we formed during college years but because we have taken the time to build lasting, lifetime friendships. We get together several times each year, often with our families at special events, and annually for a weekend at our farm. We work at staying close.

When I decided to run for Congress, several of my fraternity brothers and teammates from the computer industry volunteered to help. Some joined the campaign full-time, putting their lives on hold for several months. They camped out in a modest motel, working from dawn to nearly midnight seven days a week. My wife, Patty, our children, Kent Jarrell and Ann Eppard from my computer company, and others joined us as we tramped from door to door throughout the ten counties of the district. Kent and Ann put together a dazzling computer system that churned out thousands of personalized letters to the homes we had visited. Fraternity brothers Dave

Green and Tom Jenkins led the crew at headquarters, fielding que-
ries, scheduling events, writing press releases, and clipping papers.
Eddie Basch took on the job of acquiring and refitting an old school
bus with desks, seats, and a loudspeaker from which marching music
blared. Ed painted the bus red, white, and blue, with "Bud Shuster
for Congress" signs on the sides. My "little brother," Mark Nagy, gave
us his family car, and his father became my campaign chairman. Bill
Greenlee provided invaluable professional TV, radio, and newspaper campaign advertising, along with opposition research. Uncle
Herman and Aunt Margaret manned the house and the mimeograph
machine.

On Election Day, dozens of Sigma Chi brothers, computer buddies, our nieces and their sorority sisters, converged on the 9th Congressional District to work the polls. One nasty newspaper ran a picture
of us gathered at our victory party, titled "Strangers in the Ninth." But
they were not strangers to me. They were friends and family.

Years later, when I suffered my broken neck and was facing a
series of dangerous operations, my Sigma Chi "big brother," Dr. Joe
Marasco, a world renowned radiologist, traveled to the farm to spend
time with me, assuring me that he had carefully studied the X-rays
and that the dangerous surgery was required. Although I was supposed to be in the midst of a competitive campaign, I had to watch
from the sidelines while my staff and supporters, led by my chief of
staff, Ann Eppard, pinch-hit for me. (I won by a landslide, or more
accurately, *they* won by a landslide!)

Seek out friendships that have the potential to last a lifetime,
and work hard at not only having true friends, but at *being* one.
Once I was criticized by some Pittsburgh Republicans for hosting a
fundraiser to support Lloyd Fuge, a Democratic candidate, for a judge-
ship. But Lloyd was my college debate partner and fraternity brother.
My response was immediate and direct: He's my friend.

Be prepared, however, for disappointments. Few friendships
last forever. You will be fortunate if, beyond your family, your true
lifetime friends exceed the fingers on your hands. Friends can drift
apart, interests can change, and conflicts can arise.

One of my most painful experiences occurred when a close high-school friend and I went off to Pitt together. We were "rushed" by Sigma Chi, and had our hearts set on joining that fraternity. I received a bid, but he did not. I had taken the measure of the other rushees at the various events and knew that my chum was as good or better than most. It was an unfair, rotten rejection. I can recall the tearful experience that took place in my attic bedroom. I hugged him and told him that I didn't want to be a member of a fraternity that wouldn't include him. They were elitist and no damn good! Yet, I knew I still wanted to accept their bid. Even though I had received bids from other fraternities, I had decided from the very start that there was no other fraternity for me. *We* had decided that together we would become members of the best fraternity on campus...in the world!

He said that I would be foolish not to join, that we could still be friends. "Don't pass up this opportunity. Don't be dumb," he protested.

I *grieved* over the dilemma, and though I have always felt a tinge of guilt about my decision, it turned out to be one of the most important of my life. (When I became president a few years later, we eliminated the single "black-ball" system!) The fraternity opened doors for me at the university: I could not have achieved my student leadership positions without it. That would have meant no Senior Award, no counterintelligence opportunity, no computer-industry job, no Washington, D.C., experience, probably less financial security, no Congress, no Shuster Lodge, and almost none of the lifelong friendships I have enjoyed.

My experience as president of the Inter-fraternity Council, coupled with my visits to fraternity houses on my debate trips, taught me that the quality of any fraternity or sorority experience depends on the particular chapter at any given time. Carefully evaluate the specific circumstances before you leap.

It's also important not to confuse true friendship with the veneer of friendship—cordiality or collegiality. We delude ourselves when we mistake a business relationship for friendship, even though it can be both pleasant and productive. When I arrived in Congress, a wise senior member, Congressman William Hungate of Missouri, told me, "Young man, you're going to see lots of friendly people around here, but very few friends."

When people are brought together by mutual interests—working toward a common goal, living nearby, participating in the same activities—they get to know each other and are courteous and cooperative. They benefit from the relationship. But when there no longer is a mutual benefit to the relationship, it fades and disappears.

It's important to carefully measure the quality and durability of blossoming friendships. Too often, I've witnessed people being hurt by their so-called friends. Friendships based on mutual economic or political interests are especially susceptible to eventual conflict. I've seen managers and political leaders support the career advancement of subordinates, only to have them become disloyal to advance themselves. Employees with whom managers thought they had a bond of friendship, left, stealing customers or confidential data. A few congressional staffers have run against the member who gave them their start.

I promoted a salesman into management once, only to have him later bad-mouth me to my boss in an attempt to get my job. Fortunately, it offended my boss. I took no pleasure in firing the salesman, but it was important to forcefully demonstrate to our hard-working, loyal employees that there was no room for backstabbing in our organization. Disloyalty should rank as the eighth deadly sin.

Confusing friendship with a professional relationship can be dangerous. Unless you're secure in the durability of a lasting friendship, never tell a friend anything you wouldn't want him to know if he became your enemy.

In a modern-day parable, Michael Eisner and Jeffrey Katzenberg grew up together on Park Avenue in New York, and when Eisner became head of Paramount Studios, he brought in his friend, Jeffrey, as his assistant. Later, when he became chairman of Disney, Katzenberg came with him. For two decades they worked together making movies—and millions of dollars. But when Eisner promoted another man to be president, their friendship soured. Katzenberg sued the company for $200 million, claiming he had been underpaid. Under oath, Eisner admitted that he recently had stated, referring to his one-time friend: "I think I hate the little midget!"

Probably the most devastating of broken bonds occurs when love turns sour, when one is rejected by another. Sometimes, the rejection comes from "falling out of love." The fire goes out. People change. Sometimes it is caused by circumstances beyond one's control.

In Sir Walter Scott's *Ivanhoe*, Rebecca is told she cannot marry Ivanhoe because she is Jewish. In anguish, she cries out to her father, Isaac, "My heart is broken and I cannot live without him," to which Isaac replies, "My heart has been broken many times, and I live...I live."

If we are shattered by the broken bonds of friendship, love, or family, we can either shrivel up, burning with self-pity and animosity, or look forward, with the passage of time, to embracing the many other bonds that still exist. Sometimes the best decision is to redouble our efforts to repair the broken bonds, for true friendship, love, and family are too precious to be lightly cast aside.

Wherever life takes you, no matter how you may temporarily trip and fall, remember that you are indissolubly linked to your family and your true friends by a firm chain, the links of which should only be broken by death. Your joys, your sorrow, your afflictions all are shared by them. When your heart is sore, your faith weak, and your courage nearly gone, remember that there are bonds of love and affection embracing you from which to draw consolation for the past, comfort for the present, and hope for the future.

Let your whole life be such that when it is time to cross the final river, you will be able to say, "I have been worthy of my family, my country, and my friends."

* * *

My dear Grandchildren,

My hope is that this book will help you add extra meaning to your life. And many years from now, when I am a distant memory—when you are alone in the stillness of the night or standing silently in the black walnut grove beside the river at the farm or, perhaps, walking along a seashore half a world away, you will close your eyes and listen closely. In the rustling of the leaves, or the lapping of the waters, only for an instant, will you hear me whispering in your ear: *Grandy loves you...Grandy loves you...Grandy loves you.*

Bud Shuster at his boyhood home in Glassport

Grandy's Life

E. G. Bud Shuster, known affectionately as "Grandy" by his grandchildren, was born January 23, 1932, in Glassport, Pennsylvania, a steel valley town fourteen miles south of Pittsburgh. He graduated magna cum laude from Glassport High School, where he earned a varsity letter on a championship basketball team (always insisting he was the poorest player on the team). He performed leading roles in school plays and played the piano in high-school concerts, as well as at a roadhouse that reportedly doubled as a house of ill repute (the knowledge of which he always denies).

Winning an academic scholarship to the University of Pittsburgh, he graduated Phi Beta Kappa in 1954 and was named "Outstanding Senior," a distinction for which his name was chiseled on the campus walk. At Pitt, he won the Grand National Debating Championship and served as president of the senior leadership society, Omicron Delta Kappa, Sigma Chi fraternity, and the Inter-fraternity Council. He was the cadet colonel of the university's ROTC regiment.

Along the way, he worked as a ditch-digger, railroad gandydancer—spiking down railroad ties—movie-house usher, floor scrubber, washtub emptier, amusement-park-ride operator, shoe salesman, car washer, night watchman, storekeeper for an Indian tribe in the Canadian North Woods, and a college Camel cigarette promoter, for which he is more embarrassed than playing piano in a reputed bawdyhouse.

Bud with his mother

Bud goes to
Boy Scouts camp

Bud at Lake George, New York

Upon graduation from Pitt, he entered the U.S. Army, wearing the cross-rifles of an infantry lieutenant. After attending combat intelligence and counterintelligence schools, he became a counterintelligence agent.

He married Patricia Rommel, with whom he had five children: Peg, Bill, Deb, Bob, and Gia.

In 1956, after an honorable discharge from the military, he joined the UNIVAC computer division of Sperry Rand, progressing through computer programming schools, eventually becoming the company's national account manager to the United States Steel Corporation. During that time, he discovered that even as the teetotaler he was then, he could put down Manhattans with hard-drinking steel executives by gulping down sixteen ounces of buttermilk before joining them for their liquid lunches. In the same period, he learned other, perhaps more productive lessons, earning an MBA from Duquesne University at night.

In 1960, Shuster left the computer industry for a year to become field sales manager for the Photostat Corporation in Rochester, New York, before returning to Pittsburgh as district manager for RCA's computer division. He later was promoted to vice president of government marketing for RCA's computer division in Washington, D.C., earning a PhD in business from The American University in his spare time. He left RCA to become president and chairman of a small, ailing computer-terminal company, as well as a founder of a computer software company, but sold his interests in both companies before returning to Pennsylvania to run for the 9th District Congressional seat in 1972.

He was elected to fifteen terms in the U.S. House of Representatives, winning not only the Republican nomination, but also the Democratic nomination, nine times on a write-in ballot, a feat never before accomplished in Pennsylvania's history. He also was elected a delegate to six Republican National Conventions and served as a co-chairman of the platform committee three times.

In Congress, Shuster served as chairman of the Transportation & Infrastructure Committee, the largest committee in congressional

Bud at graduation from the University of Pittsburgh

history. He shepherded into law TEA-21 in 1998 and AIR-21 in 2000, the historic highway-transit and aviation acts. He also produced the Water Resources Act to restore the Florida Everglades, the largest environmental restoration project ever enacted, and numerous other major pieces of transportation, economic development, water resources, and disaster-relief legislation.

As the ranking member of the Select Intelligence Committee, he authored legislation to strengthen U.S. intelligence capabilities, including "Robin Quart," a then-classified air-to-ground surveillance operation that was instrumental in bringing down Columbian drug lords and knocking out Iraq's command and control systems during the 1991 Gulf War. He had the honor of being presented with a captured Iraqi battle flag by the Robin Quart soldiers, who sustained no casualties in their daring operation behind enemy lines.

At the recommendation of the U.S. Command, as the war was about to begin, he participated in a press conference aboard the USS *LaSalle* in the Persian Gulf and "let slip" his understanding that the U.S. invasion would commence with a massive amphibious landing by the Marines on the east coast. This disinformation reportedly played a role in causing Saddam Hussein to concentrate his forces on the east coast to repel the supposed attack, allowing U.S. forces to sweep around his west flank in the desert.

Shuster was a driving force behind the creation of the Counter Narcotics Center at the CIA.

By meeting clandestinely in Moscow with Elena Bonner, wife of atomic scientist and Soviet dissident Andrei Sakharov, he was able to help smuggle Sakharov's famous "Letter of Conscience" written while he was a prisoner in Gorky, outside of Moscow, to the free world.

As president of his 46-member GOP freshman class during Watergate, he was asked by the White House to hold together the freshman class in support of Richard Nixon, dining privately with the president aboard the presidential yacht, *Sequoia*, a month prior to Nixon's resignation. Although he had the difficult duty of informing the president that a majority of Republican freshmen, including himself, would vote to impeach him, his constructive role in the painful process was praised by William Timmons, legislative director of the White House, who wrote in a letter for publication: "To his credit, Mr. Shuster did not exploit his position as a leader of the new Members to gain media attention, as he could have during those explosive days. Because his counsel remained private, reasoned, and candid, I feel he was one who played a significant role in that ultimate outcome when the President resigned for what he felt was best for the country."

Congressman Shuster served as chairman of the Republican Policy Committee, as a member of the Budget Committee, a delegate to NATO's North Atlantic Assembly, and a trustee and trustee emeritus of the Kennedy Center.

He has received more than 130 awards for his congressional service, an honorary Doctor of Laws degree from St. Francis University, the Bicentennial Medallion of Distinction from the University of Pittsburgh, where he served as a trustee, and a special award from the Central Intelligence Agency for his contribution to national security.

He was named by the prestigious *Congressional Quarterly* as "one of the five top legislative drivers in Congress." (The other four were senators.)

The *National Journal* reported, "Shuster has chalked up a remarkable record. Not surprisingly, his colleagues regard him as one of the last great chairmen on Capitol Hill."

In a speech honoring Chairman Shuster, Speaker of the House Dennis Hastert said: "Bud, because of your leadership and determination, we changed the way we do business around here...you really changed the face of America."

Upon his retirement from Congress in 2001, he became president of Strategic Advisors, serving as a consultant to several corporations, chairman of Safe Extensions, Inc., a producer of patented lighting systems for airport runways, and a visiting professor and trustee at St. Francis University, where his congressional papers and memorabilia are being archived and displayed. In 2003, Juniata College named its new environmental center, overlooking Lake Raystown, Shuster Hall.

His son, Bill, was elected to his 9th District seat.

Bud and Patricia Shuster reside on a farm named Shuster Lodge, in Bedford County, Pennsylvania. Carved into a stone at the entrance to Shuster Lodge is an S inside a seven-dotted circle, symbolizing the seven members of the family protected by the circle, with space between each dot to signify the individuality of each member. Inscribed below are the words: "Dedicated to those who came before who built so we might thrive." They have set aside an acre for each of their grandchildren.

Shuster is the author of several articles on transportation, economic development, and national security, and five books, including the award-winning *Believing in America*, three novels, *Double Buckeyes, Secret Harvest, Chances,* and now this "Love Letter" written for his grandchildren—and parents and grandparents—everywhere.

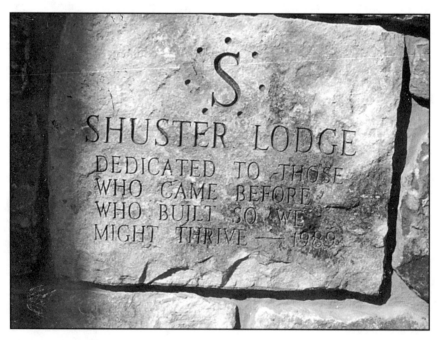

Inscription beside front door of Shuster Lodge